REDISCOVERING
CATECHISM

REDISCOVERING CATECHISM

THE ART OF EQUIPPING COVENANT CHILDREN

DONALD VAN DYKEN

P&R
PUBLISHING
P.O. BOX 817 • PHILLIPSBURG • NEW JERSEY 08865-0817

Scripture quotations are from The Holy Bible, New King James Version. Copyright © 1979, 1980, 1982, Thomas Nelson, Inc. Italics indicate emphasis added.

Page design by Tobias Design
Typesetting by Michelle Feaster
Cover design by Now You See it!
Cover photo, "Remember the Sabbath-Day, to Keep it Holy." Courtesy of the
Billy Graham Center Museum.

Printed in the United States of America

Library of Congress Cataloging-in-Publication Data

Van Dyken, Donald, 1940–
    Rediscovering catechism : the art of equipping covenant children / Donald Van Dyken.
        p. cm.
    Includes bibliographical references.
    ISBN 0-87552-464-8 (pbk.)
        1. Catechetics—Reformed Church. 2. Reformed Church—Catechisms. 3. Christian education of children. I. Title.

BX9428.A1 V36 2000
268—dc21

00-055063

Contents

Preface   vii

1. A Tale of Two Cities   1

2. Anchoring in the Past   5

3. The Meaning of Catechizing   11

4. The Meaning and Place of Catechisms   17

5. The Importance of Catechism   25

6. The History of Catechizing: Moses to Paul   35

7. The History of Catechizing: Alexandria to Massachusetts   43

8. An Encouraging Word   49

9. Covenantal Catechism   55

10. How Shall We Teach Catechism?   65

11. Teaching Catechism: Memorizing and Questioning   71

12. Teaching Catechism: Review and Repetition   77

13. Teaching Catechism: Learning and Singing Songs   85

Contents

14. Who Is Taught? Who Teaches? 91

15. Putting a Program Together 97

16. Catching a Catechist 103

17. Battle Proven 109

Appendix A: Selected Confessions and Catechisms 115

Appendix B: Publishers and Bookstores 133

Notes 139

Preface

This book is written to aid in the renaissance of catechism, particularly to revive the catechetical method of training children. The art or perhaps we may say the grace of catechizing has been a potent force in the history of the church.

This book is addressed to readers whose churches teach catechism but perhaps are unaware of its principles and history, to those whose churches have dropped catechism teaching, and to those who are unfamiliar with the concept. This book addresses all who hold their children dear, love the church of Jesus Christ, and greatly long to see the extension and expansion of Christ's kingdom.

The book covers two general areas. Chapters 1 through 7 investigate the meaning and history of catechizing; chapters 8 through 17 outline practical considerations and steps for productive catechizing. Since each section is largely self-contained, you may turn to either section first. It is my prayer that the Lord, through this work, will excite in his churches that indomitable spirit of conquest that characterized the "saints who nobly fought of old."

For whatever is unworthy in this work I take full responsibility. For whatever is true and worthy I wish to acknowledge my debt of gratitude to all the little and big children it has been my joy and privilege to catechize these past twenty years; to my late and beloved father, the Reverend Harry Van Dyken, a man of the covenant and of great compassion, and a catechist nonpareil; and above all to my faithful God and Father, who through Jesus Christ has always cradled this poor sinner in his covenant love with such incredible long-suffering and faithfulness.

Chapter 1

A Tale of Two Cities

"It was the best of times, it was the worst of times." So Charles Dickens opens his *Tale of Two Cities,* a historical novel of London and Paris in the days of the French Revolution. His words also describe our times.

Although our times are bad enough, it will not do for Christians to moan and wring their hands. History is full of bad times when God called up men and women of strong faith and glorious deeds, and we must prepare our children for that call. The best means to fulfill that duty, as this book will try to convince you, is by returning to catechism teaching, a method of instruction in biblical truth that the church has used for centuries.

In the first two chapters we will do some groundwork. First, we must be sure that our confidence is in Christ. Second, we will see that Christ is leading churches today back to the biblical model of teaching the Word through careful questions and answers. Third, we'll note that families are reclaiming their children from the world. Fourth, we'll see that we can firm up and safeguard these gains if the church and the family will join hands. Fifth, we'll note that if we return to the Christian heritage of catechizing children in the truth, the church may well look ahead to a faithful and victorious future.

THE GOOD OLD DAYS ARE NOW

Only in such an atmosphere of sober biblical optimism does a return to catechism fit so well. However, since you are swimming against the rising tide of moral degeneracy and anti-Christian activism, you will probably need convincing proof.

In the first body of evidence we'll consider, God testifies about his Son in relation to our own time and tomorrow. Today is the best of times because Jesus Christ is King of kings and Lord of lords (Rev. 1:5). Our Redeemer rules upon the throne at the right hand of God. By him the universe was created (John 1:2); by his law all things are ordered and upheld; by his blood he is redeeming his people from every corner of the world. It is the best of times because God witnesses that Christ shall reign until all his enemies are crushed (1 Cor. 15:25).

Is Christ reigning now? Looking at the top of any page of your newspaper may, paradoxically, reassure you. The news media may sometimes irritate or enrage us, but they chronicle, unawares, a daily fact that many Christians overlook. Every page gives the date—the day, month, and year. The date reminds us that this is "the year of our Lord." We have a daily reminder of the reign of our Lord Jesus Christ.

It is the best of times because as this King governs the affairs of mice and men, he orders all things for the benefit of his church (Eph. 1:22–23). He numbers our hairs (Matt. 10:30); he knows more about us than we know of ourselves. This powerful Redeemer-King holds his people in his hand and has promised that no one can snatch them out (John 10:28). Therefore, if we must go through what seems the worst of times, we are held in the best of all hands, inseparable from the best of all loves (Rom. 8:38–39).

Those are the facts as God reports them in his Word.

They testify, don't they, that we live in the best of times? We should appreciate our need for encouragement. The world outside and the old man inside attack us daily, wear down our hope, and slow down our efforts. Only when God realigns our hearts to these grand eternal truths are we strong again.

Remember the incessant opposition that confronted Moses, David, and Paul. Their strength and perseverance caught breath again only through their vision and grasp of eternal Truth. Imparting that vision and grasp to the rising generation is the target of catechizing.

THE TALE GOES ON

It is the worst of times, and it is the best of times. For today as always, history is the tale of two cities, the city of man and the city of God, Babylon and Jerusalem, the world and the church. The battle between the two continues, but the outcome is never in doubt.

While we live in the worst of times, let us embrace what is best. Let us take the invincible truths of almighty God, pour them into the minds and hearts of our children, and send them forth into the field of battle.

Let us join the Calvin of the Reformation and say, "We who aim at the restitution of the Church, are everywhere faithfully exerting ourselves, in order that, at least, the use of the Catechism . . . may now resume its lost rights."[1]

In the next chapter we will see how Christ is moving the hearts of his people today.

Chapter 2

Anchoring in the Past

Two developments in the church and one in the home present great potential for the future if Christians will but grasp the opportunity at hand. That opportunity is to reconnect the church to its past and forge links into the future.

BACK TO THE BASICS

We should all be greatly encouraged that many churches have been formed by believers who have left drifting churches. They have separated themselves from those whose theology and life have played tagalong with the world. They have sensed that the church has cut itself adrift from the historic faith. Therefore as churches have labored to realign themselves with the Scripture, to get back on track as it were, they have returned to the Reformation and the early church.

Another pilgrimage has begun of late. Tiring of feel-good, man-centered worship and sensing that feelings do not generate truth but that only the truth can generate reliable feelings, many people seek to return to ordered worship and ordered living, hallmarks of a doctrinally stable church. Many Christians are weary of antinomianism and understand that God did not move from a law-orderly Old Testament to reveal a disorderly Christ.

By reclaiming Luther's grand discovery of justification by faith, Christians again embrace the law with David, Paul, and James. The law leads to Christ, plainly outlines the extent of Christ's payment, defines his righteousness, protects believers from sinning against God's love, and enables them to give concrete expression to their love for God by deeds of obedience. This again is a return to historic Christianity, to the historic church.

RECLAIMING OUR CHILDREN

One further development today is pregnant with promise for the future, and that development is home schooling and Christian schools. If you are attracted to this movement, you have grasped an essential covenant concept, whether or not you believe in infant baptism as the historic church has. For the covenant concept teaches that God sets apart children of believers and on the foundation of his promises expects the covenant home and church to nurture them in his Word and ways. (Chapters 8 and 9 expand on the truths that adhere to a biblical understanding of the covenant of infant baptism.)

You have seen that the public school system has failed, that its stated or assumed premise that your children belong to the state is false, and that the philosophy undergirding its teaching is anti-Christian. Turning from that you have seen that the Lord gives us children in trust and that he expects us to teach them all things in the light of his Word. As you have gone through the trials of home schooling or setting up a Christian school, you have found and appealed to God's promises about your children.

The evidence, then, is that believers are leaving decaying mainline churches; others are disillusioned with the circus atmosphere of many modern evangelical churches. Both are returning to find union with the doctrine, worship, and God-ordained order of the historic church. Paradoxically yet biblically, as believers are turning to the past, they are also looking to the future. They are thinking generationally. The hearts of the fathers are returning to their children (Mal. 4:6).

LINKING IT ALL

Rejoicing in that, we all should realize that when some degree of continuity with the past has been forged, we need to take steps to ensure that this union continues in the future. Faithful instruction of the next generation is the normal mechanism God employs for the advance and growth of his people.

Therefore, to assure ourselves that the gains God has thus far granted are consolidated and that our efforts to secure biblical training for our children are not dissipated, we need an organization to guard our links to the past and the future. We need an organization, a body, to unite us in the present. We will not need to make a new one but to use the one God has founded for these very purposes—the church. God describes the church as the pillar and ground of the truth (1 Tim. 3:15).

Those two metaphors, "pillar" and "ground," describe what we have been looking for. The church is rooted in the historic work of God in Jesus Christ, is built upon it, and as such is the ground of the truth. The essence of the New Testament church is that she reaches back and bonds herself to this Christ of history. For the only Jesus Christ we have is the one who in history was promised, was born, suffered, died, rose, and ascended. On that foundation the church must also be a pillar of the truth. As she maintains the purity of preaching, as she teaches—catechizing her children in the truth—she is also the pillar of the truth.

This book is written to encourage Christians to model church teaching after the biblical and Reformational pattern. As we shall later see in more detail, an indispensable component, especially in teaching children, is the practice of catechizing and the formulation and use of catechisms.

DISCOVERING LOST PATTERNS

Perhaps you have never heard of catechism. Or you may draw a blank when trying to imagine what catechizing is. That is understandable, because the vast majority of Protestants have no concept of the meaning of catechizing, or they associate it only with the Roman Catholic Church.

A few years ago John J. Murray, a preacher from Scotland, surveyed the scene and said,

> What was looked on as a necessary and beneficial practice by the early church and by the reformers has now fallen into such disuse among Christian people that very few seem to have any understanding or appreciation of the subject. *We believe it is to the discontinuance of this practice [of catechizing] that we can trace much of the doctrinal ignorance, confusion and instability so characteristic of modern Christianity.*[1]

The situation at the time of the Reformation was similar to ours. Ignorance was rampant, the truths of Scripture were unknown or neglected, and the result was confusion of mind and ungodliness of life. Lancelot Andrews (d. 1626), head of the first company of translators of the Old Testament for the King James Version of the Bible, said, "When catechizing was left out of the church, [it] soon became darkened and overspread with ignorance."[2]

RECOVERING LOST PATTERNS

What then will we try to do in this book? We want to return to the old, tried and true paths, as described by the Reverend Ronald Christy:

> There was a day in Scotland—the best days, some folk think—when a minister or a catechist gathered families together in a home and catechized them—probed their understanding and experience of Scriptural truth, encouraged them to express themselves. Such catechetical instruction was a source of spiritual strength. Where is that done now? Hardly anywhere.[3]

This book is dedicated to bringing back a potent weapon in the church's arsenal—catechism and catechizing. We should all desire that Christians united in churches once again pioneer in this wasteland of sin called modern society. Let us bring to mind the ancient glory of a church boldly charging the old Roman Empire, that stronghold of Satan. Let us recall the glorious triumphs of truth pushing back the frontiers of darkness during the Reformation.

"What we now bring forward, therefore," says John Calvin in the dedication to the *Catechism of the Church of Geneva,* "is nothing else than the use of things which from ancient times were observed by Christians, and the true worshippers of God, and which were never laid aside until the Church was wholly corrupted."[4]

Chapter 3

The Meaning of Catechizing

Catechizing is a particular method of instruction historically used by the Christian church. To germinate the idea we can imagine ourselves on a ship looking for a submarine. The submarine hides deep below the surface of the ocean. Our ship is equipped with sonar, and our operator sends out sharp sounds into the dark waters. Those sound waves travel down through the water until they hit something. Sometimes they strike a school of fish, or the bottom, or the sub we are searching for. When those sound waves bounce off the hull of that sub, the sonar device picks up the echo. From that echo the operator can get a fix on the submarine's position.

That illustration introduces us to the teaching concept known as catechizing—sending out questions and listening for the echo, the answer that fixes the depth of knowledge and understanding. When you question people, you find out "where they're at." The word "catechism" derives from the Greek word *katecheo,* which is found in several places in Scripture. The most familiar is Luke 1:4, where Luke explains why he wrote his Gospel: "that you may know the certainty of those things in which you were instructed [catechized]." Like many Greek words *katecheo* is put together from two words, in this case *kata,* meaning "down toward," and *echeo,* meaning "to sound." *Katecheo* is "to sound down."

SOUNDING HEARTS

To catechize is to sound down, to speak to someone with the objective of getting something back as an echo. Catechism sends a sound to probe a student's understanding. We use the catechetical method of questioning to send out the Word in order to hear responses, to gauge the depths of someone's knowledge, to probe the heart.

There are several places in the New Testament where the example of catechizing and the command to teach are emphasized. Apollos was "catechized" in the way of the Lord (Acts 18). Jesus commanded Peter in John 21:19 to feed his lambs. Teaching is obedience to the Holy Spirit's command through Paul to Timothy, "These things command and teach" (1 Tim. 4:11). We will explore the examples of Christ and the apostles more thoroughly in chapter 6.

ANOTHER SUNDAY SCHOOL?

You may think that if catechizing is teaching biblical truth in the church, then this book serves no purpose since most churches have some kind of Sunday school program. I would suggest, however, that with rare exceptions most Sunday school teaching programs do not fit the historical model of catechism.

The modern Sunday school movement began in 1780 by reaching unchurched children. The movement was outside the official ministry of the church, although its efforts were evangelistic and admirable. However, the Sunday school concept has been embraced by many churches but often has attained only quasi-official status. In adopting a Sunday school program for their own children, churches blurred the biblical and Reformational distinction between the children of unbelievers and the children of believers. Catechism, by contrast, is and always has been the official teaching of the church. Catechism is specifically designed to teach children of the church. We shall see more of this later.

The method employed in many Sunday schools emphasizes doing and seeing. Children color pictures, cut out characters, play games, and act out Bible stories; they are visually engaged by overhead projectors and videos. To the extent that such activities preempt teaching by *word,* we should seriously question whether they serve the biblical and Reformational model.

The biblical and Reformational model is catechizing, a method of teaching in which hearing and speaking are central. If the church needs men and women of faith for the days ahead, we must return to listening to the Word and from there to asking questions and getting answers. "Faith comes by hearing, and hearing by the Word of God" (Rom. 10:17). If we expect our children to mature, to stand fast for the truth, to contend earnestly for the faith, to resist the great deceiver, and to fight as the saints who nobly fought of old, they will need basic training more rigorous than making slingshots to understand the story of David and Goliath.

A Short Trip to the Past

A brief look at the question-and-answer method as used yesterday and today may help to illustrate some of its advantages. In a later chapter we will explore the history of catechizing in the church, but now I simply point out that the question-and-answer method is a technique effectively used by ancients and moderns both within and outside the church.

The dialogues of Plato (427–347 B.C.) record Socrates' method. He taught his disciples by question and answer, and his technique is commonly called the Socratic method. It is a variation of catechizing. Not only pagan teachers but also great teachers in church history have used the question-and-answer method to make sure their teaching was effective: for example, Augustine (353–430) in his *Catechizing the Uninstructed,* Anselm (1033–1109) in *Cur Deus Homo,* and Erasmus (1466–1536) in his *Ten Colloquies* (a colloquy is an informal conversation). Erasmus wrote his work as "a school text, a short book of formulas, question-and-answer sentences, . . . and [it] continued to be used for three centuries."[1]

The great leaders of the Reformation, Martin Luther, John Calvin, and John Knox, attacked the colossal ignorance they met in Germany, Geneva, and Scotland by making catechisms and by catechizing.

CATECHIZING IN THE NEWSROOM
AND THE COURTROOM

Although respect for journalism has declined because of biased or careless reporting on TV and radio or in newspapers and magazines, older journalists recall editors who demanded the truth—unadulterated. In a relentless pursuit of complete and accurate coverage, reporters interviewed people thoroughly. They probed, they dug, and they investigated—all the while asking questions—to find answers. That is part of the idea of catechizing.

Similarly, although we tend to view lawyers and judges more as villains than as heroes of the courtroom, our judicial system at its best makes good use of the question-and-answer method. The courts catechize to determine some of the most important issues of life: they award or fine parties enormous sums of money; they decide people's lives and liberty. To do so, they need a method that gets at the truth, and question-and-answer dialogue is such a method. Lawyers examine and cross-examine witnesses, digging and probing with questions to get at what (we can hope) is the truth.

Perhaps you can see that catechizing is not just an old or odd practice. Both today's news media and our judicial system, when at their best, rely heavily on the question-and-answer method. In a word, they depend on catechizing.[2]

CONCLUSION

Catechizing is a question-and-answer teaching method that bounces words off students, catches their responses on the rebound, and serves up words again as needed. We gain the basic concept from the New Testament and see it illustrated in history and culture.

In the next chapter we will look at catechisms—books of questions and answers—as they relate to the Bible and creeds in the practice of catechizing.

Chapter 4

The Meaning and Place of Catechisms

Throughout the centuries the church has employed good scriptural and doctrinal catechism books to ensure thorough biblical knowledge, doctrinal stability, and an effective walk before the Lord. Godly use of catechism material generates greater devotion to the Word. We have said earlier that catechisms are books written to help in the practice of catechizing, but they are more than that. Almost all catechisms spring from creeds and confessions, so we'll look at the concept of creeds and confessions to capture the principles involved.

The validity of confessions is an issue for all Christians who long to return to historic Christianity, for as they journey into the past they inevitably encounter confessions. Whether they visit the church in Hippo, North Africa, where Augustine preached, or slip into the back pew of St. Andrews, Scotland, to listen to John Knox, they will find churches that faithfully held to the Bible and as tenaciously held to creeds and confessions.

WHY NOT USE ONLY THE BIBLE?

At the outset we are confronted with an obvious question: Isn't it a mistake to add man-written books to what God has written? This question deserves serious thought, for it usually comes from people who have seen the word of men, and particularly of theologically well-educated men, imposed upon God's Word.

By considering a few instances, we can see the issue clearly. For example, when your pastor stands behind the pulpit with nothing but a Bible in his hand, what does he do? When you as a Sunday school teacher sit in your class with your Bible on your lap, what do you do? Both of you open the Bible and read; then you begin or your pastor begins to explain the passage. You show how it relates to the rest of Scripture, open up its meaning, and draw out applications for your hearers.

Or, when you visit your Christian bookstore, what do you find there? If your bookstore is typical, you'll find shelves filled with books trying to show what the Bible says about loving one's spouse, coping with teenagers, balancing your budget, witnessing to your neighbor, and every other conceivable subject.

In all of these situations, we hear and use man's words. And if we are candid, we recognize that we haven't purged all the words of man from our churches, even if we say "No creed but Christ" or "No word but the Bible."

By discarding confessions we haven't eliminated the words of men, and we have probably worsened our problem. By allowing many conflicting views in our churches, we have replaced the confessions of the historic church with the shifting currents of the times.

CHRIST COMMANDS CONFESSIONS

When Christ asked the disciples who they would say he was, Peter answered, "You are the Christ, the Son of the living

God" (Matt. 16:16). Although he could have recited Isaiah 9:6, Peter did not quote from the Bible. Instead he used his own words, and Jesus blessed him for doing so. Confessions in our own words are not only acceptable but also required. Confession defines the Christian: "If you confess with your mouth the Lord Jesus . . . you will be saved" (Rom. 10:9).

By implication confession defines the church as well. Paul admonished the Corinthian church that they "all speak the same thing" and to be "perfectly joined together in the same mind" (1 Cor. 1:10). Paul is saying, "Get your act together! Get unified on what you are going to say about Christ and the gospel!"

A confession or a creed, then, is formed when the church gathers and writes what it is going to say about the Bible, its Author, its message, and its themes—that is, what it says about God, man, Christ, and salvation. Based on that confession the church writes a catechism book that is the most proven method of teaching her confession.

A study of the great sixteenth-century Reformation witnesses to this very sequence of events—first the Word, then confession, then catechisms. The Reformation brought God's Word back to the people, the church. All over Europe these churches responded by writing creeds and confessions. Then they followed with catechisms, a natural outgrowth of a living, confessing church. Catechisms were the best way to teach the young and ignorant.

A CATECHISM BOOK JOINS HANDS

A catechism book expresses our unity in the truth, and teaching that truth to our children unites us to the future. Our catechism book may also be written in such a way that it joins us with the past. If we want to return to the historic faith, we will be entranced to find so many churches in history whose creeds and confessions bring a warm echo from our hearts.

The most important endorsement, however, of any creed, confession, or catechism book is from the Son of God, the Word incarnate. We need to be assured that Christ will say to us as he said to Peter, "Blessed are you, Simon Bar-Jonah, for flesh and blood has not revealed this to you, but My Father who is in heaven" (Matt. 16:17).

In essence catechism books express our common confession of what the Scriptures teach. We express our unity with each other in the local church, with other churches that confess as we do, and with faithful churches of the past. We join hands with Christ, with our brothers, and with the saints gone on before. But we have another direction to reach out, and that is into the future. We are happy to find out that the main purpose of catechisms is to reach our children.

CHRIST'S CONSTRUCTION PROMISE

When you as parents, teachers, or ministers reach out to your children and teach them the church's confession, one more pleasure awaits you, and it is the crowning joy. Christ in the Word confronts the church with the same question he posed to the disciples. The church answers by confession as Peter did. She receives the benediction of God upon her answer as Christ gave to Peter.

As the church teaches that same confession to her children, she may hear Christ say, "On this rock I will build My church" (Matt. 16:18). That rock is the confession of Peter, the confession and catechism of the church. Christ himself promises to build the church upon her confession.

We have seen some of the principles that lie behind the

need for catechisms: our unity in the truth and Christ's commands and promises. Reinforcement of these principles comes from two writers learned and eloquent in the Word.

ECHOES FROM THE PAST

Matthew Henry (1662–1714) was a Puritan pastor and commentator whose writings have increased knowledge of the truth, devotion to Christ, and godly walk for many generations of Christians. Henry describes a catechism book as "that which is intended in these forms of sound words [catechisms] . . . to collect and arrange the truths and laws of God, and to make them familiar." He adds:

(1) By these forms of sound words, the main principles of Christianity, which lie scattered in the Scripture, are collected and brought together. . . . Now our catechisms and confessions of faith pick up from the several parts of holy writ. . . .

(2) By these, the truths of God are arranged and put in order . . . the harmony of divine truths, how one thing tends to another, and all center in Christ, and the glory of God in Christ: and thus, like the stones in an arch, they mutually support, and strengthen, and fix one another. . . .

(3) By these, the truths of God are brought down to the capacity of young ones.[1]

BIBLICAL GEOGRAPHY

The second writer is G. I. Williamson, a faithful Christian minister and teacher who has written two fine cate-

chism study guides, one on the Westminster Shorter Catechism and the other on the Heidelberg Catechism, both
well-beloved catechisms from the Reformation.[2] Parents
and teachers may find his comments encouraging:

> . . . the catechism is something like a map. We could
> ask, "Why bother to study a map? Why not just go out
> and study the surface of the earth instead?" The an-
> swer, of course, is that one is wise to begin with a
> study of maps. After all, life is short and the world is
> very big. One person, working by himself, could only
> map a small portion of the earth's surface. That is
> why maps are so valuable. They exist because many
> people over many years have made a study of the
> earth. And while these maps are not perfect, they are
> quite accurate. Thus, the best way to begin to un-
> derstand the geography of the world is not to start
> with the world itself. No, the best way is to start with
> a good atlas. Then, after getting hold of the basics
> one can go out and test the atlas by actually visiting
> some of the places described in it.
>
> It is much the same with the Bible. The Bible
> contains a great wealth of information. It isn't easy
> to master it all—in fact, no one has ever mastered it
> completely. It would therefore be foolish for us to try
> to do it on our own, starting from scratch. We would
> be ignoring all the study of the Word of God that
> other people have done down through the cen-
> turies. That is exactly why we have creeds. They are
> the product of many centuries of Bible study by a
> great company of believers. They are a kind of spiri-
> tual "road map" of the teaching of the Bible, already
> worked out and proved by others before us. And af-
> ter all, isn't this exactly what Jesus promised? When

he was about to finish his work on earth, he made this promise to his disciples: *"When He, the Spirit of truth, has come, He will guide you into all truth"* *(John 16:13).* And Christ kept his promise. When the Day of Pentecost came, he sent his Spirit to dwell in his people. The Holy Spirit was poured out—not on individuals each by himself, but on the whole body of Christian believers together (Acts 2). And from that time until this, he has been giving his church an understanding of the Scriptures. It is no wonder that the church expressed itself from very early times through creeds.[3]

Catechisms, properly written and used, never replace the Bible. On the contrary, they direct our attention to the Bible, excite our interest in its glories, and bring together its truths. As a catechism charts the main features and outlines the grand themes of Scripture, we are led to an orderly understanding. Thus our reading and study of the Bible are more profitable, our life is more fruitful, and our praise and thankfulness to God are more intense.

May our Lord grant that the church and the home take up the task of planting the truth in the hearts and lives of the next generation, lest through neglect or selfishness we fail to endow our children with the fullness of their heritage in Christ Jesus. By the Lord's grace the ancient means of catechetical instruction can be a vital tool in this work.

Chapter 5

The Importance of Catechism

An obedience born out of love for our Lord Jesus Christ is the primary reason for engaging in any activity, and catechizing is no exception. The Scriptures tell us that children are a heritage of the Lord (Ps. 127). Our covenant God gives children to families, to Israel, and to the church of Jesus Christ. They are the heirs of the promise; "for of such," said Jesus, "is the kingdom of God" (Luke 18:16). Christ warned, "Take heed that you do not despise one of these little ones, for I say to you that in heaven their angels always see the face of My Father who is in heaven" (Matt. 18:10). A neglect of the command to teach these little ones is a grave offense.

The Scriptures also teach that knowledge is basic to faith and godliness. "Faith comes by hearing, and hearing by the word of God" (Rom. 10:17). Eternal life, said Christ, is to know the Father and to know Jesus Christ his Son (John 17:3). John J. Murray said,

> Scripture attaches great importance to knowledge and gives a foremost place to the mind and understanding. Ignorance and error are the effects of the

Fall and it is upon them that Satan's kingdom is
built. Knowledge and truth are the grand weapons
by which it is overthrown and Christ's kingdom established in the individual and the world.[1]

Satan's kingdom seems to erupt and spread everywhere. A few examples are the disarray in marriages and
families and the worldly living and the ungodly pleasures
that characterize not only the world but so often the
church. The contemporary situation mirrors what the
prophet Hosea saw: "My people are destroyed for lack of
knowledge" (Hos. 4:6).

DOCTRINAL BABES OR MEN?

Perhaps we can understand how an anti-intellectual,
antidoctrinal atmosphere has found acceptance. Christians have watched brilliant theologians mutilate, twist,
and pervert the Word of God. Disgusted with these ways of
turning the truth of God into a lie, some Christians have
eschewed learning itself, whether past or present. "Away
with theology!" they cry. "Give me the simple gospel!" But
is ignorance better than falsehood? Can the great God and
Creator whose mighty acts and wondrous character con-
front us on every page of Scripture be reduced to a scant
few beliefs?

The simplicity of the gospel is precious, but its simplicity
never robs it of its profundity. Place a rose in the hand of a
child, and that child can see that it is a beautiful, fragrant
flower, a gift of God. But place a rose in the hand of Luther
Burbank, and without losing any of his simple, child-like
wonder and appreciation for its beauty, he could devote a
lifetime exploring its profound complexity.

DOES DOCTRINE DIVIDE?

"You shall know the truth, and the truth shall make you free" (John 8:32). We could say that the more truth we understand and believe, the greater will be our freedom in Christ. "And this is eternal life, that they may know You, the only true God" (John 17:3). We could also say that the more knowledge we possess of our Triune God, the fuller and richer will be our life.

Some Christians harbor the notion that doctrine divides people. But true doctrine unites rather than divides. True doctrine teaches us about Christ, who is the Truth, the Word from above. When we teach and keep the truth about him, we are bound together in an eternal bond. The truth unites us to God and to each other.

By contrast, false doctrine divides, separating man from God and men from one another. Satan's false doctrine in the Garden of Eden separated Adam and Eve from God and later, Cain from Abel. False doctrine is the lie, and the lie has caused all the divisions this world has ever experienced.

Do we have trouble seeing the truth? We all do, and so we may promote error and contention as well. But this doesn't mean that we should abandon the pursuit of truth or yield to the world's claim that there is no truth. Although we may not possess truth fully, yet it is there to be possessed. We may fault our sinful shortsightedness for failing to see the truth, but we may not fault God for speaking it.

Sometimes, as we contend for the truth, we sin. But if we find ourselves failing to "speak the truth in love," the solution is not to forsake the truth. The solution is rather to confess our sins, bearing patiently with one another and rejoicing in the truth.

THE CHURCH OF TOMORROW

Catechism is important because the church of the future rests on the faithful instruction of God's people by parents and catechism teachers. As soon as the Reformation began, the churches built for the future. The preface to the *Catechism of Geneva* says, "One of the first and most laudable efforts of the Reformers was to revive the practice [of catechizing], and restore it to its pristine vigor and purity; and hence, in many instances, when a Church was regularly constituted, catechizing was regarded as part of the public service."[2]

From a human perspective, if the Reformers had not regarded the catechetical instruction of its children one of its foremost responsibilities, the church would not be here today. From a theological perspective, though, the doctrine of predestination fueled the great efforts at catechizing. If we remember that Augustine was the ancient champion of predestination, we'll also recall that Martin Luther's conversion occurred in his context as an Augustinian monk. Luther and all the Reformers were champions of predestination. For a God who does not predestinate is not sovereign, and a God who is not sovereign is no God at all.

If predestination means anything, it means that God reveals his plan for the future through his promises. God's promises for the continuation of his church from generation to generation were built upon his promises to work in the hearts of the children of his people through his Word and Spirit.[3] Out of faith in these promises sprang the unflagging zeal of the Reformation churches to catechize the next generation in the grand Reformation teachings of scriptural truth.

THE REFORMATION AND CATECHISM

God opened the way for the Reformation through the printing and distribution of the Bible. As you may recall, Johann Gutenberg completed the first printed book, the Bible, in 1456. By 1517 when Martin Luther posted the ninety-five theses to the door of the castle church at Wittenberg, the presses of Europe had distributed all or parts of the Bible in Latin, German, Italian, French, Czech, Dutch, Hebrew, Catalan, Low German, and Greek—truly an astounding work of God.

Following this, God raised up godly men of great intellectual and moral stature and fired them with passion to preach. The churches responded by writing confessions and catechisms, and then carried their Bibles and confessions and catechized, as Paul said about his work in Ephesus, "from house to house."

During the Reformation, catechizing commanded the interest of small and great. Frederick, ruler of the Palatinate, saw no better means than catechizing to ensure his subjects were grounded in the Reformed faith. He commissioned Olevianus and Ursinus to write a catechism. After Frederick and ministers of Palatinate reviewed it, they published it in 1563. That catechism, the Heidelberg, among the many written during the Reformation, still retains the distinction of being one of the best known, loved, and used of all the Reformation catechisms.

In 1643 an assembly of godly men equipped with enormous scholarship gathered at Westminster Abbey, London, England, and in 1647 produced the Westminster Confession of Faith, perhaps the most theologically precise and mature doctrinal formulation of the Reformation. Rather than content themselves with stating the truth, this assembly kept working. They wanted to make certain that Christ's people not only heard the truth but also learned it. To reach this goal, they employed catechism; they added the Larger and Shorter Catechisms to the Westminster Confession.

Keen observers credit catechism teaching for the propagation and preservation of the Reformation. Looking back from the twentieth century, Murray said, "Where the catechetical system of instruction was adhered to the best fruits of the Reformation were preserved and transmitted."[4]

Richard Baxter (1615–91), a minister of the Word, lived in England through the powerful counterattacks of the Church of Rome and the Arminian party. He credited catechizing as a major factor in the survival and achievements of the Reformation.[5] Three hundred years from now, should the Lord tarry, may that testimony be made of us.

The Enemies React to Catechism

The importance of catechism can also be gauged by the reaction of the enemies of the faith, and one example comes from the early church. About A.D. 312 the Roman emperor Constantine appeared to be converted to the faith. By his Edict of Milan (314) the Christian faith was officially tolerated in the Roman Empire. However, his nephew Julian, remembered in history as Julian the Apostate, succeeded him. During his time church schools throughout the Roman Empire taught children, catechizing them in the faith. But on June 17, 362, Julian the Apostate decreed that no teacher could stay in those schools without government certification.[6] By that means he intended to eliminate catechizing. In the providence of God he met his death the next year in battle. But it is striking that an enemy of the faith would recognize how instrumental catechizing is, while so many professed believers do not.

Another example comes from the Reformation. The Church of Rome convened the Council of Trent (1545–63), specifically to arrest the progress of the Reformation. The council observed, "The heretics [by that they meant the Protestants] have chiefly made use of catechisms to corrupt the minds of Christians."[7] "The papists . . . acknowledge," said Lancelot Andrews (1555–1626), "that all the advantage which the Protestants have gotten of them hath come by this exercise [of catechetical instruction]."[8]

A powerful force that arose within the Church of Rome was the Society of Jesus, or the Jesuits, to reclaim the losses incurred by the Reformation. Ignatius Loyola, Francis Xavier, and five other men organized the Society in Paris in 1537. In 1543 Pope Paul III gave them his blessing, and in time they became the greatest missionary and teaching organization in the Church of Rome. The first effort of the Jesuits was to set up religious schools for the young. They catechized rigorously. "Catholic and Protestant historians are agreed that it was by this religious school machinery that the Jesuits arrested the Reformation in its onward and apparently triumphant advances."[9] Even today Jesuit schools occupy a place of academic eminence.

The Roman Catholics learned well by noting the success of the Protestant catechizing. Although as the years passed, the proper use of catechizing fell into decay among many Protestant churches, the Church of Rome, at least during the nineteenth century, still recognized its power.

PROTESTANTS LAYING DOWN THEIR ARMS

H. Clay Trumbull, in a massive survey of catechizing, recalled this conversation in the 1800s.

A Roman Catholic priest was visiting an Episcopal bishop of the United States. The Episcopal bishop was supposed to be Protestant and the priest said to him, "What a poor foolish people you Protestants are. You leave the children until they are grown up, possessed of the devil, and then go out reclaiming them with horse, foot, and dragoons. We Catholics, on the other hand, know that the children are as plastic or clay in our hands. We quietly devote ourselves first to them. When they are well instructed and trained we have little to fear for the future."[10]

The church today has largely abandoned the catechizing of its children, and we need not strain our eyes to see the fruit. Ignorance and apathy rule in their hearts. Colleges flood their minds with illusions. They hear an old tune and recall the lyrics of rock songs heard years before, while the words of *A Mighty Fortress* are strangers to them. Mom and Dad wonder where their children went, but they are gone forever. Yet,

> if young people are to make confession of faith intelligently and sincerely, they must be well informed. For the sake of our churches and for the sake of our members, our churches have ever worked for thorough indoctrination. The catechism class has been the main means of indoctrination in the past. Catechetical instruction is indispensable to the welfare of our Churches.[11]

A share of guilt for the decline of catechizing rests on church leaders. William Shedd in *Pastoral Theology* said, "In the whole range of topics in pastoral theology there is not one that has stronger claims upon the attention of the cler-

gymen than the doctrinal instruction of the rising generation."[12] Again he said, "We feel deeply that there is not a
subject of greater interest than the catechizing of the
younger generation."[13] However, too many seminaries
downplay or ignore the art of catechizing.

WRAPPING UP

If Christ's parting commission to the church is "to make
disciples" (Matt. 28:19), she cannot fail to begin by catechizing her own children. To do less is to neglect our own
household, which Paul says, makes us worse than an infidel
(1 Tim. 5:8). If we as parents would be faithful to our calling
as the primary teachers of our children, then catechizing
should be a priority in our homes. If our greatest heritage is
the truth of Scripture we have received in trust from God
through the Reformation, we as teachers and pastors can do
no less than to return with devotion to the catechizing of
our children and youth. To do less is to deny the value of
that precious faith of our fathers.

It is the unanimous testimony of the Reformers of the
sixteenth century, of those who saw the faith of the Reformation survive the onslaughts of a century of fierce opposition, and of many commentators on Reformation history,
that a key element in God's gracious formula for victory was
catechetical instruction. The enemies of the Reformation
united in asserting that catechetical instruction was the major force in securing the Reformation in the minds and
hearts of the people.

In military operations, although planes and tanks boast
speed and firepower, it is the infantry that covers territory,
wiping out pockets of hidden resistance and securing the
conquest. Catechetical instruction is that infantry.

Chapter 6

The History of Catechizing: Moses to Paul

In the physical world of toasters and computers, we lay out spreadsheets and fix breakfasts today because of what others discovered and built yesterday. We are all connected to the past, to history, even though it may fail to interest us. In the spiritual realm of words and learning, however, a disinterest in history and a refusal to learn from the past may put us in the spiritual poorhouse and our children begging on the streets. We turn then to the past to learn what God has done in and through his people.

ISRAEL

Beginning at the time of Moses, Israel, in common with the civilizations of that time, had few books. Teaching then relied heavily on two factors that history tells us were strongly developed among peoples of limited literacy. The first factor was an accurate memory for the spoken word. Without notes, reminders, books, computers, calendars, or other aids to memory, early peoples had an amazing ability to retain information.

A second factor, closely related to the first, was oral teaching. If one cannot teach from a book in one's hand or with sophisticated teaching aids, one has to rely on hearing and telling, on asking and answering questions.

As Moses gave his parting instruction to Israel, he said, "These words which I command you today shall be in your heart. You shall teach them diligently to your children, and shall talk of them when you sit in your house, when you walk by the way, when you lie down, and when you rise up" (Deut. 6:6–7).

Moses was God's prophet, or preacher, and his preaching was a declaration. As faithful preachers deliver a sermon today, Moses spoke the words of God, without interruption or discussion. For the application of that sermon, however, Moses told parents to adopt a slightly different method, and that was familiar (family) discourse—talking with the children about the Word of God.

In addition, Moses appointed the Levites to an important role in teaching. The Levites were God's ministers,[1] and they were assigned places throughout all of Israel.[2] They seemed to have a place in every house,[3] and their role included teaching.[4] With parents and Levites working together, we see the beginning of formal catechetical teaching.

THE JEWS AND THEIR SYNAGOGUES

By the time Christ was born, synagogues had been built not only in many towns of Galilee and Judea but also throughout the world. Although worship still concentrated in the temple, the main purpose of the synagogue was for study and teaching of the Word. Schools for teaching the children were established in the synagogues, and children from five to ten years of age were taught in these schools[5] with the Bible as the only text. The method of instruction was almost entirely catechetical, that is, by question and answer. "The idea of attempting to instruct passive hearers does not seem to have entered the acute Jewish mind."[6]

At age twelve a Jewish boy became Bar Mitzvah, that is, a son of the law. When he was twelve, Jesus went with his parents to the feast at Jerusalem. Later, says Luke 2:46, they found him in the temple, sitting in the middle of the teachers, listening to them and asking them questions. The astounding fact was not that a twelve-year-old boy was asking these doctors questions. Anyone familiar with the synagogue schools would know that the Jewish method of instruction was catechetical. "After the teacher had announced his theme, the scholars in turn asked different questions, which he frequently answered by parables or counter questions."[7] It was not astounding that Jesus was asking questions of the rabbis, but, as Luke records, "all who heard Him were astonished at His understanding and answers" (Luke 2:47).

THE TEACHING MINISTRY OF CHRIST

As Christ began his earthly ministry, Matthew 4:23 records that "Jesus went about all Galilee, teaching in their synagogues, and preaching the gospel of the kingdom." Teaching and preaching are closely related, and in some ways the meanings overlap. Yet Scripture makes a distinction. Preaching, as we said earlier, is primarily declarative, while teaching is more instructive, involves interaction with the hearers and is concerned with applying the truth to the understanding of the hearers.

It is significant that Jesus revealed himself as a teacher. He said to his students (disciples), "You call Me Teacher and Lord, and you say well, for so I am" (John 13:13). Of the ninety times Jesus was addressed in the Gospels, sixty times he was called Rabbi or Teacher.[8] In Matthew 22 we find an interesting example of question and answer. "Teacher," said the Sadducees, "Moses said . . ." and then came their question about the resurrection. After Jesus answered them, a lawyer had a question: "Teacher, which is the great commandment in the law?" After he answered, Jesus turned to the Pharisees and engaged them in questions and answers about the meaning of Psalm 110:1.

In these examples we see that preaching and teaching went hand in hand in the ministry of our great Prophet. In the apostolic age we shall see this same partnership.

THE TIME OF THE APOSTLES

The word "apostle" means "ambassador" and implies preaching, for an ambassador is not first of all interested in discussing his proclamation but in announcing it faithfully. He comes from the court with the word of the great King. But to think the work of an apostle ends with proclamation is to miss what Jesus said in his commission: "Go therefore and *make disciples [learners]* of all the nations, baptizing them in the name of the Father and of the Son and of the Holy Spirit, *teaching them* to observe all things that I have commanded you" (Matt. 28:19–20).

If we understand that preaching is a declaration of the truth and that teaching, although similar, is to ensure that the hearer has fully grasped and understood the truth, we will know why the apostles began their ministry "daily in the temple, and in every house, they did not cease *teaching and preaching* Jesus as the Christ" (Acts 5:42).

Similarly, at Antioch Paul was *"teaching and preaching* the word of the Lord" (Acts 15:35). At Thessalonica he *"reasoned* with them from the Scriptures" (Acts 17:2). To the Ephesian elders he said he *"proclaimed* [the Word] to you, and *taught* you publicly and from house to house" (Acts 20:20). Finally, at the end of his ministry Paul in Rome was *"preaching* the kingdom of God and *teaching* the things which concern the Lord Jesus Christ" (Acts 28:31).

Thus it is not surprising to hear Paul say to the minister Timothy, "A servant of the Lord must [be] . . . *able to teach"* (2 Tim. 2:24). Again, as Paul sees his own work, he charges Timothy, *"Preach* the word! Be ready in season and out of season. *Convince, rebuke, exhort,* with all longsuffering and *teaching"* (2 Tim. 4:2). And as Paul looks ahead he says, "The things that you have heard from me among many witnesses, commit these to faithful men who will be able to *teach* others also" (2 Tim. 2:2).

WHEN TEACHERS DO NOT TEACH

Paul here lays down a fundamental truth. In the previous paragraph we quoted Paul describing his work as a partnership of preaching and teaching. In Ephesians 3:7–9 he says, "I became a minister . . . that I should preach . . . and to make all [people] see." That is, his task is to preach and to teach, but instead of using the word "teach" he uses the phrase "to make all [people] see." In doing this he defines teaching as making someone see the truth. We might restate his comments as a fundamental axiom: *Teaching is not only telling the truth but also making someone know the truth.*

Using that axiom as a starting point, we may then say that many teachers do not teach. Instead, they lecture. Let's take the subject of "Justification by Faith Alone" as an example. A teacher may present the subject, develop it, support it, show its relation to sanctification, and give an hour-long speech. But that person has not taught if he is unaware of whether his hearers have grasped the subject. We fall short of fulfilling the role of a teacher if our students fail to know what we have presented. We judge the teacher by measuring his students' knowledge rather than measuring his own knowledge or delivery. Has the matter penetrated their minds? Can they recall and rehearse what they heard?

The Long Way Round Is the Shortest Way Home

We have a convenient word to help us create the proper image of a teacher, and that word is "doctor." The word "doctor" originally meant anyone who was especially learned and could indoctrinate others in his learning. "Doctor" meant also "teacher," and the teaching or the subject matter he taught was called doctrine.

If our young daughter wakes up with a terrible pain in her lower right side, we take her to the family doctor; he is a doctor of medicine and knows what treatment or medicine to give her. Recalling that "doctor" means "teacher," we know that this doctor does more than tell us what he knows. As a teacher he brings his knowledge to bear on his student, the patient. His fingers gently probe her side; he listens for and feels her reaction. His fingers tell him that her abdominal skin is taut and hot. He puts a thermometer under her tongue to check her temperature. He wraps a band around her arm and checks her blood pressure. He draws a sample of blood from her arm and sends it to the laboratory.

"Yes," says our doctor, "she has acute appendicitis, and we will need to operate at once." So this teacher continues to apply his knowledge to his student. As the anesthetics, the scalpel, the sutures, the antibiotics, and the painkillers are applied, the doctor has his patient monitored, hourly, daily, until she returns home.

Does all that probing, testing, and monitoring sound like the questioning of the catechetical method? Catechizing, instruction by the question-and-answer method, is the proper way to fulfill the role of teacher—not merely lecturing and telling the truth, but catechizing, applying the truth to another, the medical doctor to his patient, the truth doctor to his student. By implying that to teach is not only to tell the truth but also to make someone know the truth, Paul has led us to the doctor's office. And by providence our reference to Paul brings us home, for his constant companion, the beloved physician, Luke, first introduced us to the idea of catechizing (Luke 1:4).

Chapter 7

The History of Catechizing: Alexandria to Massachusetts

THE EARLY AND MEDIEVAL CHURCH

The early church stressed the importance of teaching and soon established the office of teacher or catechist. The church at Alexandria, Egypt, founded a school, perhaps the greatest of all institutions of learning in the early church, which was specifically known as a catechetical school.[1]

Augustine (353–430), known then as a great preacher, today as the great theologian of the doctrine of grace, has also been called "one of the doctors of the universal church."[2] Building on our understanding that a doctor is a teacher, we are not surprised to hear that he prepared a book entitled *Catechizing the Uninstructed*, in which he detailed the steps in the process of wise catechizing.

In history most of us leap from 500 to 1500, from Augustine to the Reformation, thinking of the thousand years from the fall of the Roman Empire to the Renaissance as a nondescript fog called the Dark Ages. Few lies have been more successfully perpetrated by Renaissance humanists than this one. We must note, however, that the churches of Jesus Christ did not cease to teach during this great period of expansion and building. Nor must we lose sight of many vigorous teaching programs established throughout Europe.

A canon attributed to the Sixth General Council of Constantinople (680) promoted setting up charity schools in all country churches, since they were already found in all city churches.[3] From what we may know about monasteries (which regrettably may be little indeed), it is clear most of them began by setting up schools. Charlemagne (d. 814) vigorously promoted the cause of education throughout his empire. "To aid this educational program Charlemagne drew scholars from wherever he could find them. They came from Ireland, Spain, Italy, Gaul, and, notably, England. In the seventh and eighth centuries some of the Anglo-Saxon monasteries had become centers of learning."[4]

Beginning about 1380 the Brethren of the Common Life established schools throughout the Low Countries and Germany for children and for adults as well. Other faithful forerunners of the Reformation allowed no child to grow up without being able to give an account of his or her faith.[5] These were the Waldenses (c. 1100–1500, followers of Peter Waldo in Southern France), the Wycliffites (c. 1380–1500, John Wycliffe and the Lollards in England), and the Hussites (John Huss, d. 1414, in Bohemia). The "Waldenses demanded that the children should be taught in the Holy Scripture and the doctrine of faith."[6]

The Reformation Church

One of the first efforts of the Reformers was to return sound catechetical instruction to the churches. In Geneva under the leadership of Calvin the whole catechism was covered in fifty-five Sundays, the children regularly coming forward to be questioned by their pastor.[7] Calvin said that the children must be carefully trained at home by their parents and had to attend Sunday catechism classes.[8]

One of Luther's early efforts was to write a catechism for teaching the young and ignorant in the principles of the Christian faith. According to F. V. N. Painter in *Luther on Education,* "Education remained through Luther's whole life a cherished interest."[9]

The great Reformer of Scotland, John Knox, wrote in his *Book of Discipline* that the minister must take care of the children and youth of the parish, instructing them in the basic doctrines and especially in the catechism.[10] The General Assembly of the Church of Scotland provided that the second service each Lord's Day include the catechizing of the young and ignorant.[11]

Of this period we may say that all the Reformers (Luther, Melanchthon, Calvin, Zwingli, Beza, Knox, and Cranmer) and all the churches supported catechism teaching faithfully.

AFTER THE REFORMATION

In 1618 to 1619 the Synod of Dort[12] was convened by the States-General of the Netherlands to resolve the Arminian controversy. Delegates were invited from the Protestant churches of many countries, and some of the early sessions were devoted to catechism. The president of the assembly, Johannes Bogerman, introduced the discussion pleading the indispensability of this labor, particularly, since, as he pointed out, the Jesuits were taking great pains in catechizing children and youth. The delegates then shared their own catechism practices and views with the assembly.

The English judged that schoolteachers should drill the children in catechism every week and that on Sunday the catechism should be recited. The men from Hesse, Germany, recommended that elders everywhere prepare lists of baptized members eight years old and up and make certain that members attend catechism classes. Delegates from Emden, East Netherlands, reported that children of five and six recited questions without hesitation and children of eight and ten knew the complete catechism. Finally the synod adopted various measures to ensure catechism teaching would continue in full strength among the churches.

"Sweet Land of Liberty"

The Pilgrim fathers had fled from England and settled in Leyden, the Netherlands. Although they expressed full agreement with the conclusions of the Synod of Dort, they wanted to preserve their English heritage. Gaining permission from the English monarch, they sailed from Holland to found a colony in America. In 1620 they landed at Plymouth Rock.

Others followed, and it is reliably reported that the three basic books to be found in the majority of early New England homes were the catechism, the Psalter, and the Bible.[13] The schoolmaster drilled the children in catechism, and the people recited the catechism yearly in the church. Although this is part of America's pilgrim heritage, today ninety-nine out of a hundred Americans fail to know what catechism means.

This sketchy history of catechism, of the teaching ministry of the church, may convince you that it has been an integral part of the church's program in both Old and New Testaments. Faithful churches throughout history have maintained it, God revived it during the Reformation, and I pray he may revive it again today.

Chapter 8

An Encouraging Word

Children are a heritage from the LORD. (Ps. 127:3)

In this chapter we'll move from talking about catechizing to practicing it. After we look at some of the troubles we may encounter, we'll pause while the Holy Spirit strengthens our hearts. Finally, I'll gently remind teachers that their most important asset is the gift of a great love.

Since we want the effect of our catechizing to be evident in our children many years from now,[1] we must realize that we are undertaking more than finding a little clearing in the child's mind and quickly setting up a tent. There are acres of trees and brush to be cleared, stones to be dug out, foundations to be laid, and a permanent house of truth to be erected in our child's mind and heart. An illustration will help us see the magnitude of the challenge of going from planning to performance.

ONE STEP AT A TIME TO THE TOP

Planning the climb of a great mountain demands time and effort. There is an exhilarating pleasure, however, in poring over maps, choosing clothes and hiking boots, and packing candy bars and tents. As we busy ourselves in preparation, once in a while we pause and imagine for an instant the glorious moment ahead, standing at the top, astride that snowcapped peak, all the world spread out at our feet and the long trail winding below.

The day comes, however, when we have safely packed our plans in our minds, hoisted our backpacks to our shoulders, and started climbing. Although careful planning and packing are essential to our success, what we need now is strength, endurance, and perseverance. Fallen logs, brush-choked paths, swollen streams, and rising cliffs all block our way. As the days wear on, our legs wear out, the blood pounds in our ears, and all we want to do is quit. But we must push on. The summit belongs to those who overcome.

THE OPPOSITION

Catechism teaching stretches out longer than a five-day assault on Mount Shasta. Let's consider the difficulties. They are dumped in our path by children, parents, ourselves, the world, and the devil. The devil hates not so much us or our children but the truth. He is the great opposer, and his greatest efforts are put forth in opposing the truth and in keeping it from our children.

Children can be stubborn, slow to learn, inattentive or disinterested—although disinterest usually is the result of ignorance. If parents are too busy or reluctant to make sure their child knows the lesson, the child will reflect that indifference in class. If parents show indifference by failing to take time out during the week to check up on their child, their sin may be visited upon their child (Exod. 20:5).

Sometimes, if the church doesn't provide catechism classes, parents willingly accept this responsibility. In other instances, some parents may complain about the inconvenience of bringing the children to catechism, or that their child does not fit in the class, or that the lessons are too hard. Soccer practice, basketball games, school essays, and vacations all clamor for priority over catechism. Another obstacle may be too much time spent on watching television, which numbs children's minds, dulls their sensitivity to sin, and warps their perception of truth.

A teacher may find that he is inadequately prepared, loses patience, or forgets his goals; in short, he sometimes walks by sight instead of by faith. He finds his own weakness blurring his vision, for whenever we put ourselves under the microscope, we look less competent than we are. To cure this weakness, it is wise for the teacher to turn from himself to the lesson material.

Delving deeply into the subject and exploring Bible truth reveals glory upon glory. Biblical truth is what we teach. God and his Word will unfailingly yield new beauties upon closer examination.

In over twenty years of catechism teaching I have encountered all the obstacles described above. But, happily, we can face them together: parents, children, teachers, and God. He overcomes, and we through him. As a result, looking back I see a long line of eager children maturing into godly Christians. And behind them, the beauty of teaching mothers and dads raising sons and daughters of the King.

BLESSEDLY BAPTIZED

Imagine you are with your class. Picture the little fellow in the front row, the one with his shoelaces loose and his eye and hand following the fly on the table. Seven years ago his parents carried him to the front of the church to be baptized by the minister.[2] As the minister sprinkled water on the young lad at the command of Christ, God in a very personal way performed at least two gracious acts.

First, he demonstrated that the blood of his beloved Son has power to cleanse the very source of all the sins this child will ever commit—his polluted heart. That is not only a wonderful demonstration, but it also carries with it a promise. To be sure, baptism lays a heavy responsibility upon the child, for he must answer this personal touch of God. He will answer—either by faith and obedience or by unbelief and wickedness. Unbelief, however, must not be allowed to obscure the rich assurance baptism provides both for the child and for parents and teachers who are entrusted with his spiritual welfare.[3]

In addition, God writes, as it were with his own finger, his name upon the forehead of the child: the name of the Father, the Son, and the Holy Spirit. God claims children of believers as his own by right of purchase (Ezek. 18:4; 1 John 1:12). He appoints and anoints parents (Deut. 6:7) and church (John 21:15) to teach them.

Therefore, just as faithful parents respond to God's claim on their children by bringing them forward for baptism, so too they may respond to God's commandment to instruct them by believing God's promise:

> And all your children shall be taught by the LORD,
> And great shall be the peace of your children.
> (Isa. 54:13)

So as home and church with trembling try to faithfully instruct the Lord's children, God himself—Father, Son, and Holy Spirit—promises to will and to work in them according to his good pleasure.

With faith in almighty God, we, like pioneers of old,

each year must grasp the plow handles, lay bare the furrow, and plant the seed. We cannot allow ourselves to be daunted by the untamed wilderness of our children's hearts or dismayed by the weeds that spring up in their lives. And let us not fear the arrows of a savage world. "If God is for us, who can be against us?" (Rom. 8:31).

By saying this, I'm not suggesting that you have faith in your child or student, in yourself, or in your church or your catechism program. Nor does God. Instead he commands us to have faith in him—Father, Son, and Holy Spirit—to trust his promises.

TRUE LOVE

Love is the basic ingredient of the catechism teacher's recipe. In 1 Corinthians 13 Paul listed many things we could have or do, but without love, he said, we make an empty noise. This then—for teachers, fathers, mothers—is the royal law of catechism: Love God and love your child or student (neighbor).

Love God because he is your central focus. The Bible is the revelation of God in Jesus Christ. Thus we teach of the One we love, the Word made flesh. We must love what we teach, for the God we teach is the heritage of children. This Jehovah who is our God is their God as well.

Children are rarely fooled. If we do not show a deep love for the Word we teach, and if we do not throw ourselves into the task of inscribing that Word in their hearts, they will see that we are putting in time at the treadmill, and the best they will do is plod the required number of steps too.

Love your neighbor, as well—your children and students. Children can be so eager, so open, so honest, so simple, and so beautiful. Jesus said, "Take heed that you do not despise one of these little ones" (Matt. 18:10). John—"the disciple whom Jesus loved"—evidently could find no greater term of endearment for Christians than "my little children." But the way to genuinely love these children we teach is by the way of faith. We can see them as precious objects of God's favor because we believe God when he says that they are his heritage.

So then, the simple meaning of catechism is this: to bring our children, who are the heritage of the Lord, to the Lord who is the heritage of our children. Our children then will love catechism, the subject and the teacher. And one of the finer joys grace affords us is the love of a little child.

Chapter 9

Covenantal Catechism

Catechetical instruction should be covenantal, or to say it differently, relationship-oriented:

- God has placed the children we teach in the covenant of grace, a very special and favorable relationship to him.
- God requires us to teach our children the meaning and requirements of that relationship in and through his covenant Word, the Bible.
- God then demands that his covenant children make a response, a confession of faith and obedience in answer to this Bible teaching.

CHILDREN IN THE COVENANT OF GRACE

In teaching our children we must view them and talk to them the same way God does. He makes clear that he views children of the covenant as those to whom he brings his redemptive word and work. God's salvation through the flood and in the exodus clearly shows that he embraces children. When he reached into the world with his only begotten Son, God did not shorten his embrace, for Jesus literally took little ones into his arms. And his apostle John said, "Little children . . . your sins are forgiven you for His name's sake" (1 John 2:12).

We must be careful not to allow a confused notion of regeneration and election to keep us from speaking of covenant children the way our heavenly Father does. We should be comfortable telling them about the glory of their Father in heaven.

Covenant children are those whom God has given to believing parents. Those parents came to be believers as God spoke to them through his Word. Through his Word and Spirit he created saving faith in their hearts. Their response to his Word and Spirit was to answer, "Yes, Lord, we believe. We believe what your church has confessed about your Word."

The desire of parents and church is that God will use the same pattern to bring covenant children to a saving knowledge of Jesus Christ. Thus, we first tell them what God says to them by teaching them the Bible. When it is time for covenant children to respond, we remind them of what their parents have said. Because these parents have embraced the words of the true church of history, we thus teach covenant children the confessions.[1]

We teach first the Bible and then the confessions; the Bible because it is God speaking to his people, and the confessions because they are the church speaking to God, answering his Word.

TEACH THE COVENANT WORD OF GOD— THE BIBLE

To teach the Bible is to give children their inheritance. They inherit God himself, for his Word says, "I am your God, and the God of your children." In all of Bible teaching we must remember that we are catechizing in the Word, in the Truth. This must always be very personal, for we are not aiming to produce a tribe of precocious Pharisees who can list biblical facts and lay out the five points of Calvinism but never know their Savior. Rather, in the Word and Truth they meet and come to know the persons of their God: Father, Son, and Holy Spirit. The Word *is* Jesus Christ. "And this is life eternal, that they may know You, the only true God, and Jesus Christ whom You have sent" (John 17:3).

TEACH THEM TO KNOW GOD

When we talk about knowing somebody, we mean more than knowing who he is (the postman is Mr. Palachio) or knowing things about him (the Prime Minister likes pizza). When a boy says, "I know my dad," he says something much deeper and much closer.

How then can our children know God? We can understand the process by watching Henry, the boy who lives down the street, come to know his dad. Henry was born into a relationship with his parents. He is growing up in their daily presence. They talked to him before he could talk; they feed him, live with him, and love him.

When Henry is six you may see him following his dad across the yard. You chuckle and say to your spouse, "Look at that kid, honey. He walks and talks just like his dad." The reason is not hard to find. It's not that young Henry is a budding actor who just completed a two-year drama course at the community college. He is a child who grew up in the cradle of covenant love, seeing and hearing his dad.

Similarly, we teach a child to know God by letting him see God work and hear God explain what he is doing. And knowing God begins with the Bible, which is the revelation of the person of God. "In the beginning God created the heavens and the earth," so we take our children by the hand and lead them through Old Testament history—at least four thousand years of the works and words of our God. Then, like a child at home, they are not so much studying God but watching him and listening to him. That is the path to intimate knowledge.

This approach to teaching our children does not begin with systematic, analytical knowledge; that may come later. Our children first gain covenant knowledge, for in the covenant, God takes them by the hand and lets them see him in action. As they see and hear him, they know him. They know his character—his power, wisdom, mercy, faithfulness, patience, holiness, love, plans, anger, redemption, and salvation. They come to know the mind of God—what he does, how he does it, and why he does it. They learn what he likes and what he does not like. In short, they get to know their heavenly Father.

Then, not merely doctrinal statements but a personal relationship birthed from Old Testament sacred history leads them to Christ. "O foolish ones," said Christ, "and slow of heart to believe in all that the prophets have spoken. . . . And beginning at Moses and all the Prophets [the entire Old Testament] He expounded to them" (Luke 24:25, 27). The way to the Christ of the New Testament is by way of the Old Testament. "This is the book of the genealogy of Jesus Christ, the Son of David, the Son of Abraham" (Matt. 1:1). The Old Testament presents us with the same God who so loved the world that he gave his only begotten Son. His dealing with Israel was with a people related to us. We belong to Israel. Paul told the Greek Corinthians that the Israelites were their fathers (1 Cor. 10:1).

When, through catechizing our children in the Old Testament, God has brought them into an intimate knowledge of his mind and ways, they are ready to grasp doctrinal matters. To illustrate this, let's take two doctrinal subjects: unconditional election and covenant baptism.

The doctrine of unconditional election teaches that God—apart from our action or merit and of his own free will—takes the first step to call certain persons to salvation. This formulation will not be foreign to children schooled in the Old Testament, for they will realize that Adam, after he sinned, didn't find God but God found him. Abraham didn't call God but God first called Abraham. Israel didn't choose God but God chose them.

How does Old Testament history illustrate covenant baptism? A critical question might be, Does God in his ordinary working include children in the unbelief or faith of their parents? Here we put the catechetical method to work and ask our children these questions: Did God curse only Adam and Eve or did the curse come upon all their children as well? Did God save Noah alone through the flood or was his family included? Whom did God drown in the flood? Just the unbelieving parents or their little children as well? Did God just deliver the adult Israelites from Egypt or did he deliver them by entire tribes and families? Our children's knowledge of God's ways will provide them with ready answers to these questions.

Continuing on then with the doctrine of the covenant—the truth that God includes children in the unbelief or faith of their parents—we lead our children to the ministry of Christ. We are not surprised then that he healed the daughter of the Canaanite woman, not because the girl had faith but because her mother did. Christ's apostles continued this pattern. When Paul addressed the church at Ephesus, he called them "saints." Because Paul spoke by the inspiration of the same Spirit who inspired Moses, we are not surprised that children are included among those saints (Eph. 6).

Let's summarize the importance of bringing our children into an intimate relationship with God through catechizing in Bible history. Today there are more false gods and idols than there were during Elijah's time. There are more false Christs than there were in the apostle John's time. Because of this it is important for covenant youth to know their God—Father, Son, and Holy Spirit. The sure method for identifying the counterfeit is having an intimate knowledge of the real God himself. "Grow in the grace and knowledge of our Lord and Savior Jesus Christ" (2 Peter 3:18).

Thoroughly and rightly understood, the Old Testament will lead our children to the New Testament, give them an understanding of the Christ, and open to them the teaching of the apostles.

FROM WHAT PERSPECTIVE SHALL WE TEACH?

Obviously our teaching of the Bible will be different than that of Roman Catholics or Mormons, and we do not pretend to teach from a neutral position, for there is none. The teacher must believe what he teaches; the first qualification is that the teacher is a child of God by faith in Jesus Christ through the regenerating power of the Holy Spirit.

A second qualification is that we teach the Bible from the framework, or perspective, of the church's confessions. In other words, we teach it from a particular doctrinal viewpoint. That is nothing to be embarrassed about, for everyone teaches from a particular doctrinal position. The question is whether the doctrinal position is itself derived from the Bible as a whole.

The Nicene Creed, for instance, is a doctrinal statement. It says that Jesus Christ is

> the only-begotten Son of God, begotten of his Father before all worlds, God of God, Light of Light, very God of very God, begotten, not made, being of one substance with the Father; by whom all things were made; who for us and for our salvation came down from heaven, and was incarnate by the Holy Spirit of the virgin Mary, and was made man; and was crucified also for us under Pontius Pilate; he suffered and was buried; and the third day he rose again according to the Scriptures, and ascended into heaven, and is seated at the right hand of the Father; and he shall come again, with glory, to judge both the living and the dead; whose kingdom shall have no end.

This doctrinal statement, gathered and distilled from the whole Bible, summarizes the truth about the person and work of Christ. If we teach from a doctrinal, confessional perspective, all our teaching will harmonize with that truth.

A COVENANT RESPONSE

When we teach our children, our desire is that they will give a covenant response. To better understand this concept, we may think about how our children learn to talk. At first they imitate sounds, sometimes combining these sounds in their own ways. As we listen, we also make sounds, sometimes gently correcting our children, and as they grow older we intentionally teach them our language.

Similarly, we teach our children how they should respond to biblical, doctrinal teaching. And the Bible leaves no option—God orders Abraham, the Israelites, and New Testament church parents to command their children to believe and obey (Gen. 18:19; Deut. 6:6–9; Eph. 6:4). So too the church, who Paul says is the bride of Christ and the mother of us all, teaches her children to answer their heavenly Father by repeating her teaching after her.[2] That means her children should repeat her confession, what the church as a true bride today and throughout history has spoken to her Husband, her Lord, her God.

From the years of teaching our children what God says, we now teach them how to answer God. Those answers come from the confessions of the church, so that our children may know how to answer the God who has spoken and speaks to them.

However, when we make the transition from teaching Scripture to teaching the confessions, we'll want to remember some important points.

- The catechumens are moving from God's Word to man's word.
- Yet they must know that God's Word demands an answer and we will be studying that answer.
- Their answer must be in union with or agreeable to God's Word, in union with the historic Christian church, and in union with the church where God has placed them.
- They must know that although we will teach them the confessions of the historic church and their own church, desiring that they make this confession their own, they must still personally give account to God for their confession. We do not believe our confessions because the church teaches them but because God's Word teaches those truths.

I sometimes tell my catechumens that if I were a Mormon and they accepted my teaching and then presented it to God as their answer to his Word, he would grade it with an F and that would mean hell. "So," I say, "although I will teach you the Heidelberg[3] with the greatest confidence that it faithfully reflects God's Word, you must personally know that it does. It reflects God's Word not because I say so, or because the church says so, or because the Reformation said so, but because God says so. You must know your Bible. If you do not, you cannot confess with honesty."

WRAPPING UP

The content of the church's catechism program should consist of two parts: imparting to our children the knowledge of the Scriptures and leading them to become familiar with the confessional answer of the church past and present.

Under the promised blessing of God, we look forward to seeing them arise in the congregation and take their stand, confessing their faith in the Word of their God in unity with the saints who have gone on before and united to the saints who yet are pilgrims waging the good fight of faith.[4]

Chapter 10

How Shall We Teach Catechism?

In chapter 3 we discussed the meaning of catechizing, and we know that it is teaching by way of question and answer. But sometimes it is a little hard to grasp what that means, and in this chapter an example will give form to the idea. Although this example focuses on a minister in a classroom, other teachers and parents can adapt the method to their situations.

A Catechizing Sampler

The minister is teaching class 2. The students, or catechumens as they were called in the time of Augustine and in the time of Luther, are about seven or eight years old. They belong to families of the church and have studied their lesson at home. The elders have told their parents that they must make sure their children know the facts of the lesson and do the required memorization, reading of Scripture, and the lesson.

(It is seldom that the children I teach fail to know their lesson, for their mothers and fathers really love the Lord, and so teaching these children by the catechetical method is always a joy.) Class 2 is partway into the study of the Old Testament. This lesson is based on Genesis 3, the account of the fall of Adam and Eve. (As you read the responses, you'll understand that these answers come from several students.)

Minister: *"Well, class, we are learning about God in Old Testament times. Do you think God was very merciful in the Old Testament?"*

Student: "No, I don't think so. I mean, he drowned all those people in the flood, and he told Israel to kill all those people in Canaan, didn't he?"

"Maybe we'd better find out what mercy means. What do you think?"

"Well, isn't mercy like being sorry for somebody?"

"Let's look at our lesson. What did God tell Adam about the tree of the knowledge of good and evil?"

"God said he wasn't supposed to eat from it."

"What did God say would happen if he did?"

"He said they would surely die."

"When would they die?"

"God said that they would die that very day."

"What did Satan say?"

"He said they would not surely die."

"Whom did Adam and Eve believe?"

"Satan."

"What did they do then?"

"They ate from the tree."

"What happened then?"

"They became friends of Satan."

"Did anything else happen?"

"Well, I don't know. What do you mean?"

"Did God do anything to Adam?"

"No, I don't think so. Did he?"

"Did Adam and Eve deserve to have something happen to them?"

"Oh, I know. They deserved to die because God said that if they ate of the tree they would die, and they knew it, and they still ate, didn't they?"

"You're right. They did deserve to die right then, didn't they? But God didn't make them die, did he?"

"No, he didn't. Oh, now I know. That was mercy, wasn't it?"

"That's excellent. Now you know what mercy is, don't you? Mercy is when God does not give you what you deserve because of your sin."

By using this method it's easy to keep the attention of little children, for if they have learned the facts of their catechism lesson at home, they love to answer questions. It's also quite easy to fill productively an hour, for we can go on with Genesis 3 about the significance of Adam in hiding and covering himself with fig leaves. We can talk about God coming to Adam, not the other way around, about the wonderful promise of Genesis 3:15, and about God's wonderful provision of a covering for Adam and Eve through the death of one of the animals.

CATECHIZING, NOT LECTURING

Scripture tells us that Christ and the apostles went about preaching and teaching. In chapter 6 we saw that these are similar but are not the same. Teaching is not merely telling the truth but also causing another to know the truth. Augustine testified that the wise catechism teacher labored to make sure that his students knew and understood the truth, not merely heard it.

At this point we should mention that some ministers tend to preach instead of teach the lesson in class. But if we remember the meaning of the terms "catechism" and "catechizing," we recall that to catechize means to sound down, to project words toward someone to gauge and measure the depth and breadth of knowledge and understanding. The catechist sends questions as probes into the heart. Well-crafted questions open hearts and expand minds.

The nineteenth-century churchman John Henry Newman understood the heart of catechizing:

> Truth, a subtle, invisible, manifold spirit, is poured into the mind of the scholar by his eyes and ears, through his affections, imagination, and reason; it is poured into his mind and is sealed up there in perpetuity, by propounding and repeating it, by questioning and re-questioning, by correcting and explaining, by progressing and then recurring to first principles, by all those ways which are implied in the word "catechizing." . . . the catechist makes good his ground as he goes, treading in the truth day by day into the ready memory, and wedging and tightening it into the expanding reason.[1]

Among the Jewish synagogue schools of Christ's day the ability and readiness to ask questions fittingly, as well as to answer them correctly, were deemed an indispensable qualification of a teacher. In the early church both Origen and Augustine placed the question-and-answer method first as an effective means of instruction. Both the Reformers and the Puritans promoted catechizing, teaching by means of question and answer. The New England Puritan preacher Cotton Mather summed it up well: "If you will be at pains . . . to instruct them in the interlocutory way of teaching, which we call catechizing, you have the experience of all ages to make you hope that vast will be the consequence, vast the advantage."[2]

THE ART OF CATECHIZING

As we approach the task of catechizing we must see that it can be a daunting task. The eminent seventeenth-century Scottish preacher Samuel Rutherford said, "There is as much art in catechizing as in anything in the world."[3] In our time John J. Murray said, "The reason why many people regard catechizing as a slight and trifling exercise is that they confuse the practice with the mere rote-work of asking and answering questions in a catechism."[4]

Catechisms, or study manuals that set out questions and answers for memory, were primarily and fundamentally designed as a help to the practice of catechizing, not as a substitute. When catechumens memorize answers from the catechism book and when the teacher asks those questions in class, the questioning has only begun. Do our children understand what they have memorized? Do they know the truth? This must be the teacher's passion, and if it is, he will persist in asking questions until his goal is reached. Although some readers may disagree with Richard Baxter when he said, "I must say that I think it is an easier matter by far to compose and preach a good sermon,"[5] we must allow that the proper catechizing of God's children presents a far more formidable challenge than many people realize.

As elder and minister I have taught catechism for twenty years, yet I consider myself far from being a wise catechist. Indeed, when I approach a class of young children, the thought hovers in my mind, "They're only kids." But Christ tells me, "Take heed that you do not despise these little ones" (Matt. 18:10).

In the next chapters we'll look at some of the means we can use in catechizing. These means include proper preparation by both the catechist and the catechumen, teacher and disciple. Proper preparation requires reading, study, and memorization. Class work—catechizing in practice—requires questioning the memory work, delving into the understanding, requestioning, rephrasing questions, reviewing, repetition, and singing. We'll explore each of these elements and offer some practical suggestions to make catechism joyful and fruitful.

Chapter 11

Teaching Catechism: Memorizing and Questioning

In earlier chapters we've seen that catechetical teaching means causing someone to know the truth by the use of questions and answers. By knowing the truth we do not mean a temporary intellectual acquaintance but "knowing" in the biblical sense, meaning a deep and intimate union or bond of love that produces fruit. Two effective tools to reach this goal are memorization and questioning. The two complement each other, and parents ensure the first, while the catechist ensures the second.

CORN AND CATECHUMENS

Sometimes people criticize structured catechism teaching by saying, "With all your requirements of reading, learning, memorizing, testing, and demanding thorough preparation, you are trying to take the place of the Holy Spirit. You cannot make believers of children. You cannot teach the Bible as you teach biology."

It is true that we cannot make believers of our children, and it's good to be reminded that we are but men and that the blessing of God and the power of the Holy Spirit alone change hearts and lives. That should keep us humble and prayerful. However, if we know the apostle Paul, we will be convinced that he spared no amount of laboring and striving, preaching and teaching, pleading and argument if by any means he might save some.[1]

An analogy from farming will clarify the point. When we walk in the field we confess that the Spirit alone gives life to our corn crop.[2] But the Holy Spirit has been pleased to bind himself to means. We do not get 180 bushels of corn to the acre by pulling out a lawn chair. Instead we pray and plow, disc, fertilize, plant, irrigate, spray, and cultivate. *Ora et labora,* pray and work.

Just as in the natural realm we are bound to use every means consistent with the sound agricultural principles that God provides to ensure a good crop, so it is also in the supernatural realm. We must use every means consistent with sound biblical principles to ensure a crop of fruitful children of God. And then we may truly say with Paul, "I planted, Apollos watered, but God gave the increase" (1 Cor. 3:6).

Getting Ready for Class

One of the reasons why teaching catechism need not be just a lecture is that we expect the catechumens to prepare by reading and studying the lesson and the Bible passages assigned. We also tell them to memorize, because memorization is an important part of preparation. Parents soon find that learning by heart is easy for some children and very hard for others. I have known mothers who had to spend half an hour every day for six days before their children knew the lesson. But once the lesson was learned, the children truly knew it and remembered it.

Some people cling to the notion that memory work is a relic of the precomputer age, that it is worthy only of parrots, and that most of the time children do not understand what they have memorized. Our survey of history, however, showed us that memorization has held an honored place in the history of the church. Memorization is remembering, and one of God's repeated rebukes to Israel was that they so soon forgot the "works" and "wonders" that he had shown them (Ps. 78:11).

By contrast, the history of the church is full of evidence that wherever true religion flourished Christians committed the truths of Scripture to memory and required children to memorize them as well. We mentioned it earlier, and it bears repeating, that in 1618 the churches of Emden, East Netherlands, reported that toddlers of five and six years old recited the principal catechism questions without hesitation and children of eight and ten knew the complete catechism.[3]

Matthew Henry lists various spiritual advantages to memorization and concludes, "Let not the wisest and best be ashamed to repeat the words of their catechism, as they have occasion to quote them; but let them rather be ashamed who cannot do it."[4]

Granted, memorization is work. It is disciplined and applied work, ill suited to a people who only do what feels good or what will pay. But have we forgotten the high cost Christ placed on discipleship?

What about the objection that children do not understand what they memorize, and that it is far better for them to know what it means than what it says? If children do not begin by knowing what it says, they shall never know what it means. Answers memorized are like the lumber used to build a house. The carpenter must measure, cut, and plane. So the catechumen comes to class with the raw material of the answers stocked in his mind. The teacher then reaches into that material and by questioning shapes it, planes it, and fits it into place.

SHAPING THE MATERIAL

As any catechism teacher can attest, a child who has faithfully memorized material will delight to have that material drawn out with questions and to explore its meaning with the teacher. But if a student has failed to memorize the material, then there is nothing stored in his mind for the teacher to pull together, and the student will quickly lose interest.

In the home parents have many opportunities to draw out the thoughts and intents of their child's heart as well. In everyday experiences, parents can help their children call up, shape, and apply what they have memorized. God has ordained these situations—in our homes, our classrooms, and our churches—in order to bring our children to a full knowledge of Christ.

To find out whether children understand what they have memorized, parents and teachers can do several things. The first and simplest is to check our children's memory work. This shows if there is material with which we can work. We can then ask questions about the lesson. Sometimes it's useful to begin a narrative of the lesson, rephrasing the memory questions as we go along. Sometimes, when we ask the memory questions in different words, we will draw a blank even if our children have memorized the answers. Then it becomes plain that our children know the answer but not the meaning.

In other ways too we can teach by questioning and by encouraging questions from our children. We can check their memory work for words they may not understand, and then we can ask about meanings. Instead of assuming that children know what they are saying, we can question what they mean. Children, especially young children, love to answer questions and then later love to ask questions.

In an hour-long class it is easy for me to lapse into lecture, except that I have on occasion been jolted by the glaze settling on my students' eyes. To avoid those lapses, as part of my preparation I make up thirty to eighty questions I can ask about the lesson and the Bible assignment. Even if I do not ask them all, that practice puts me in the questioning mode.

PREPARING TO TEACH

As catechists (in the early church this was a special office) our challenge is to catechize. This means we must engage and hold the minds and hearts of children. Our work is pastoral, shepherding lambs, and we have not finished when we have dumped a bale of hay in front of them. Augustine said that the pupil must be watched, questioned, and carefully dealt with individually; by this a student may be caused to know the truth rather than merely be caused to hear or read it.

Catechizing is a discipline, one in which proficiency comes by prayer, hard work, and practice. Discipline is expected of disciples, and in this the catechist and the catechumen share. Just as intense discipline produces good pianists, so catechists, by practice bring forth the splendid music of truth from their students.

In his *Pastoral Instructions,* John Jebb encourages teachers and parents. Jebb was a minister of the gospel in Limerick, Ireland, and although some may consider his conclusion an overstatement, it comes from a true pastor of pastors.

> Let not the common prejudice be entertained, that catechizing is a slight and trifling exercise, to be performed without pains and preparation on your part. This would be so if it were the mere rote-work of asking and answering the questions in our Church Catechism: but to open, to explain, and familiarly to illustrate these questions in such a manner as, at once, to reach the understanding and touch the affections of little children, is a work which demands no ordinary acquaintance, at once, with the whole scheme of Christian theology, with the philosophy of the human mind, and with the yet profounder mysteries of the human heart. It has, therefore, been well and truly said, by I recollect not what writer, that a boy may preach, but to catechize requires a man.[5]

In the next chapter we'll look at the use of review and repetition as catechetical tools.

Chapter 12

Teaching Catechism: Review and Repetition

A common saying among the ancient Jews was, "He who teaches without having the lesson repeated back to him aloud, is like one who sows without reaping."[1] If we adopt the principles of review and repetition, we'll concentrate on making sure that our children learn, understand, and retain the major truths of the Bible and the confessions.

CONSTRUCTING A TEMPLE

We are building a temple of truth in our children's minds. We want to set up certain truths and facts as structural members, bearing walls, and floor joists. To fix them strongly and securely in place we must review. We must pull material from our students' memories again and again, handling those materials and examining them from every angle.

If, for example, we're teaching Old Testament history, we begin again every week at the beginning and bring the accumulated knowledge to bear on the current lesson. We can vary the review each time by asking the same facts or truths in different ways. If we assume that our lesson deals with King Saul, this is one set of questions we could ask.

- What is the Bible?
- How do you know it is true?
- Why is man the greatest creature God made?
- What does it mean that God made man in his image?
- Why do all people die now?
- Who was Adam and Eve's first son? Second?
- Which one was a believer?
- What did Lamech do that showed he was one of the seed of the serpent?
- How did God save Noah and his family from being overcome by the seed of the serpent?
- Why did the people build the Tower of Babel?
- Whom did God call to keep the line of the promise going after this?
- Why could Abraham not have any children?
- Which son of Abraham was the child of promise?
- Who were Isaac's two sons?
- What does the name Jacob mean?
- What name did God give Jacob instead, and what does that name mean?
- Why did Joseph's brothers sell him?
- How does the life of Joseph show how God cares for his sinful people?
- How does the life of Joseph picture the coming Christ?
- What did Satan try to do to the children of Israel after Joseph was dead?
- Whom did God choose to deliver Israel from Egypt?
- What was the last plague?
- How many boats did it take to get Israel across the Red Sea?
- Why did God bring Israel to Mount Sinai?
- Why did God give them so many laws?
- Would Israel be saved if they kept those laws?

- Why couldn't Moses lead the Israelites into Canaan?
- Who did?
- Why did God have to send them so many judges?
- Who was the last and greatest judge?
- What does the name Samuel mean?
- Why was he given that name?
- Why do we call him a "way-preparer"?

Once we sit down to prepare and review by going over the previous lessons, we'll have too many questions to ask instead of too few.

One of my younger class's favorite methods of review is by means of a time line for Old Testament history. Drawing a line across the whiteboard, we mark 4000 B.C., 2500, 2000, 1500, 1000, 500, and 0. For each of those dates I ask the catechumens to place a name and an event showing what God did.

- 4000 B.C.: God created the heavens and the earth and Adam.
- 2500 B.C.: God sent the flood and saved Noah.
- 2000 B.C.: God called Abraham our father.
- 1500 B.C: God delivered Israel from Egypt through Moses.
- 1000 B.C.: God gave victory to Israel through David.
- 500 B.C.: God brought Israel back from captivity through Ezra.
- 0: God so loved the world that he gave his only begotten Son.

I mention these practices in order to illustrate, not prescribe, ways to realize the objective of review. The goal of review is the goal of catechizing: that our students will finish the year retaining, with ready access, the essential truths of the course. When I begin teaching the church's confessions, primarily the Heidelberg Catechism, I outline certain basic truths that (I tell my students) should forever live in the foreground of their minds. To reinforce that, I try to ask these questions once a month:

- What is a confession?
- How does it differ from the Bible?
- What are the doctrinal heads of the Belgic Confession?
- What are the five Canons of Dort?
- What does each one mean?

And from the Heidelberg, I want them to know forever:

- What is your only comfort in life and death?
- How many things are necessary for you to know, that you, enjoying this comfort may live and die happily?
- What is true faith?
- How are you righteous before God?

PACK IT TIGHT

During these later three years of confessional catechizing I want to ask these questions again and again. I want children to know the answer to the first question of the Heidelberg Catechism so well that in the terror and turmoil of Satan's fiercest attacks, in tragedy and in calm, that lovely answer may be there, cradled forever in their hearts.[2]

A story, not about the Heidelberg but about the Westminster Shorter Catechism, shows beautifully how this principle works.

In the filth and pain of the trench warfare of World War I, an English soldier stood at his post. Among the mud and sweat, the thunder of artillery, the whistling of shells, and the scream of the wounded, his face reflected a calm at odds with the chaos around. An officer noticed him and then walked past him a couple of times. Finally he stopped in front of that soldier, jabbed a finger into his chest, and demanded: "What is the chief end of man?"

The reply was instant: "To glorify God and enjoy him forever."

"Ah," said the officer, "I knew you were a catechism man."

GOD TEACHES BY REPETITION

The following are some of the teaching principles of repetition and review that God incorporated especially in Psalms, Proverbs, and Ecclesiastes. God gave us these teaching devices to aid his children in learning wisdom. The writing devices God incorporated in the Psalms are technically called mnemonic (neh-MON-ic) and didactic, meaning for memorizing and for teaching. These writing techniques are poetry, acrostics, and parallelism.

Poetry

Poetry is a wonderful aid to memory. Especially in Hebrew, all the features of poetry, such as rhythm, meter, diction, rhyme, and parallelism, are used to make the truth grip your mind and stay there. Poetry expresses the truth in a way that prose never can. Consider these words of poetry:

> He shall cover you with His feathers,
> And under His wings you shall take refuge;
> His truth shall be your shield and buckler. (Ps. 91:4)

Contrast a prose version: "God will protect you." It is true but lame compared with the poetry of Psalm 91.

Acrostics

An acrostic begins every word or line with a particular letter, whether from the alphabet or from a chosen word. For instance, the early Christian use of the Greek word for "fish" was an acrostic. The first letter stood for Jesus, the second for Christ, and so on.

Although we cannot see it in the English translation, David wrote Psalm 119 as an acrostic. The psalm includes twenty-two sections, one for each letter of the Hebrew alphabet, and within each section, every verse begins with that same letter. Jeremiah wrote the book of Lamentations on an interesting variation of the alphabetic acrostic scheme. The purpose is not just a poetic exercise; it is to aid memorization. If you've ever read William Hendriksen's *Survey of the Bible*,[3] you will notice that he is always thinking of mnemonic devices, for with a true teacher's heart he wants his readers to remember.

Parallelism

Parallelism is the principle feature of Hebrew poetry, consisting of two or more lines that express a thought in a parallel relationship to one another. The parallel expression may be synonymous or antithetical.

Synonymous parallelism occurs when the two lines mean more or less the same thing. A thought is repeated but the wording is varied so as to expand on the original idea, as this example from Psalm 119:105 shows:

> Your word is a lamp to my feet
> And a light to my path.

Antithetical parallelism emphasizes a thought by contrasting it with its opposite. Here is an example from Psalm 1:6:

> For the LORD knows the way of the righteous
> But the way of the ungodly shall perish.

Parallelism impresses upon the mind the divine content of biblical poetry. It is the hammer of repetition to fix the rivet of truth in the reader's mind. The major feature of divinely inspired poetry, parallelism helps us remember the truth by repetition and review. As disciples of the Word, we would do well to follow God's method of instruction. We can do that by faithfully reviewing the truth we seek to teach and varying the way we review ideas, constantly striving for new and better review methods to bond our children to God's truth.

Chapter 13

Teaching Catechism: Learning and Singing Songs

In 1702 the inspector of the Catholic Mission for the Conversion of the Huguenots took his job seriously, for he tortured and killed all who refused to be converted. Finally the Protestant peasants of Cevennes, France, driven and hunted like wild beasts, turned on him, killed him, and released their comrades from his dungeons. These honest mountaineers were led by Jean Cavalier, who at the age of eleven had been imprisoned for repeating something he heard in a Reformed sermon.

Cavalier was seventeen when he began leading the Camisards, as they were called, in their guerilla war of defense. By the time Cavalier was twenty-one he had routed the finest marshals Louis XIV could place on the field. When they were attacked, the Camisards fell on one knee and sang Psalm 68, arose, and rushing at the enemy fought furiously.[1] If you sing psalms in church you know how that psalm of the Huguenot Camisards begins:

God shall arise and by His might
Put all His enemies to flight. . . .

You probably sing it to the same tune as the Camisards
did, since the tune (124 in the *Psalter Hymnal*) was com-
posed in 1526.[2]

SING, YOU WARRIORS, SING

The history of the Protestant faith is the history of fight-
ers and psalm singers. In 1631 Gustaphus Adolphus, the
Lion of the North, Protestant hero and brilliant general,
led his forces of Swedish, German, French Huguenot, Scottish, and English soldiers with a mighty psalm resounding
from the ranks to batter the Roman Catholic armies of
Count Tilly.

Cromwell's army of Roundheads in the seventeenth century, patterned after his own Ironsides regiment, was mock-
ingly called "those Puritan psalm singers." Yet those troops
were never bested on the field of battle and were feared
throughout Europe as well as in England. And who shall
count the Scottish Covenanters and the innumerable company of saints throughout history who went to the rack, the
gallows, and the stake with a psalm on their lips?

Today again we need to put muscular Christians back on
the field, to fight, as the old hymn says, "as the saints who
nobly fought of old."[3] When you have catechized your children, placed the invincible sword of truth in their hands,
and engaged them in practice until it becomes an extension
of their arms, give them a song in their heart as well. Put
steel in their backbones by teaching them to sing psalms.

In "Theology and Music" Jan Smelik gives this reason for
singing psalms:

Sung praise is a mighty weapon against the devil and his powers. That is why, according to the Reformers, praise has such great value for the life of faith. Where there is singing, the devil is put to flight.[4]

CENTER ON THE PSALMS

God placed the Psalms in the middle of his Word, and they should be central in our lives as well. "What do the Psalms speak about?" asks one catechism of the children. "The Psalms speak about our awful sin, God's wonderful grace, and of our praise and thankfulness to God."[5] They speak to the heart, and from the heart of every child of God. The Psalms cover the full range of Christian experience.

When our children learn to sing psalms, they are singing the most popular music anywhere. The word "popular" means "of the people," and so a popular song is one that everybody knows and likes. We can imagine an old-fashioned scene with Grandpa and Grandma, Dad and Mom, and all the children around the piano singing. "Popular" means that everybody enjoys it, and by "everybody" I mean the whole covenant community. Popular, however, means more than this. The psalms are not only transgenerational; they bridge both time and culture. The psalms are the most popular songs in history.

When we sing "O God our help in ages past, our hope for years to come," we are singing a versified Psalm 90, written by Moses and continuously sung by the covenant family of God for thirty-five hundred years. The psalms have been translated into more languages than have any other songs in the world. Every Sunday from Argentina to Austria, from Zambia to Zillah,[6] Christians sing the psalms.

THE TOP TWO

Perhaps we wonder if our children should have something more up-to-date, in contemporary language and rhythm. For twenty years I have taught six-year-old children, and I have never met one of them who did not love to sing the genuinely popular songs, the psalms. Two songs receive the most requests from the first and second grades. Number one is from Psalm 119:

How shall the young direct their way,
What light shall be their perfect guide?
Thy word O Lord will safely lead
If in its wisdom they confide.
Sincerely I have sought Thee Lord,
O let me not from Thee depart.
To know Thy will and keep from sin,
Thy Word I cherish in my heart.[7]

The second is from Psalm 103:

The flower is withered by the wind
That smites with blighting breath;
So man is quickly swept away
Before the blast of death.[8]

Picture those eager, shining little faces singing these songs.

The psalms are poetry, and poetry is the language of vividness, learning, and memory. The psalms are also music, and music is evocative; that is, it draws out emotions. Music not only evokes emotions, but to one familiar with the songs of the faith, music also brings words into our souls. When I hear Haydn's String Quartet (opus 77, no. 1) I hear the stirring words of Psalm 98:

Sing a new song to Jehovah
For the wonders He has wrought.[9]

SINGING AND CATECHIZING

Showing you the place and practice of singing in my catechism classes will illustrate the principle of singing. (Again, I do not intend my practices to be your rules.)

The catechism books I use begin with grade 1 children. For that year and the next three, in addition to the questions and text, the children memorize one song, mostly psalms, each week. Their capacity for memorization is enormous. (The exceptions usually are children fed a diet of television, that great destroyer of memory and attention.) Each week we sing the song, and each child recites it.

Then we review. For the first ten to fifteen minutes of each class we sing their choices from the songs they already know. In that way we can easily go on (especially later) for twenty minutes and sing twenty to thirty songs. After four years and twenty-five songs a year, faithfully reviewed, these children know a hundred songs by heart. And of course, so does the teacher.

We all have to start somewhere, and the way to reach one hundred is to start with one. By making singing an integral part of catechetical training, we can muster more psalm-singing soldiers under the banner of the cross.

Let God arise and by His might
Let all His foes be put to flight;
But O ye righteous, gladly sing,
Exult before your God and King.[10]

Chapter 14

Who Is Taught?
Who Teaches?

We will help ourselves to answer the questions in this title if we first answer two other questions: (1) What is the nature of the subject matter we are teaching? (2) Whom are we teaching? Then we can ask who has the responsibility and authority to teach. In answer to the first question I will argue that since what we teach in catechism is the Scriptures and the confessions, that should properly be considered the official teaching ministry of the church of Jesus Christ. Parents entrusted with the spiritual education of their children fulfill their responsibility under the care and guidance of the church's elders.

THE BIBLE, THE CHURCH, AND THE CONFESSIONS

When we teach our children, we want them to know the Bible and the confessions. God has entrusted the Bible to the church, and what Paul says of Israel is true of the church: "to them were committed the oracles of God" (Rom. 3:2; see also Rom. 9:4; 1 Tim. 3:15.) We also find Paul saying that the ministry of the gospel is a stewardship (1 Cor.

4:1). God has committed the Scriptures to the church in trust, holding her responsible to translate it, pass it on, defend it, preach it, and teach it.

Preaching and teaching the Bible then is the official ministry and responsibility of the church. The true church has always accepted the responsibility to guard, defend, and promote the Scriptures through her official preaching and teaching. This means that the church should catechize from the Bible as part of her official teaching ministry.

Although the confessions are man's word, that does not make them either nonessential or insignificant. We do not hold them equal to the Bible, for they are a work of a different character. Where the Bible is God's Word to man, the confessions are man's words to God. The confessions are not the words of just anybody—they are both the creation and the property of the church of Jesus Christ. It follows that when she teaches them, she should do so in an official manner.

ALLOW LITTLE CHILDREN . . .

It's my position that catechism should begin when a child starts formal schooling in first grade. But because many do not accept this position, allow me to make a case for it.

Everyone except Christians seems to realize that little children are easily indoctrinated. We remember that Francis Xavier, a Jesuit missionary in the sixteenth century, was reported to have said, "Give me the children until they are seven, and anyone may have them after."[1] In our day, the television networks and their sponsors also recognize that children are impressionable! Their minds, hearts, and affections are soft and malleable.

Little children have beautiful, trusting faith, for they so often believe simply because Daddy says so or because the teacher says so. When we cultivate a relation of love and trust with little children, we make an investment. When they are young, a relatively small investment of time and effort really pays off.

By analogy, think what an investment of a thousand dollars would be worth now if we got into a booming company when it was young. That company and its stock will perish, but those who invest in little children under the blessing of God will see growth and investment returns forever and ever. To paraphrase Ecclesiastes 12: "Remember now their Creator in the days of their childhood, before the days draw near and (before we know it) their character is formed, their mind has lost its elasticity, and we can do little with them anymore."

One objection to catechizing little children is that most churches have Sunday school programs for young children, so catechism is unnecessary. (In chapter 3 we answered that objection.) Another objection stems from a misunderstanding of what catechism is. It was thought that catechism only meant the Heidelberg Catechism (or Compendium) and that it began for the youth at about age twelve or thirteen. This was the practice in Holland, and it was carried to North America. Scripture catechizing was done in schools, and later in North America the churches set up Sunday school for children aged five to thirteen. Today, however, many day schools and Sunday schools have largely failed.

For these reasons I urge the churches to begin catechism at age six. Many people, however, still think of catechism as starting with teenagers. This is mainly because many people can think of catechism only in connection with a book, such as the Heidelberg Catechism or the Westminster Shorter Catechism, but that definition is too narrow. A

catechism book is an aid to catechizing. The Heidelberg Catechism and the Westminster Shorter Catechism are aids to catechizing in church confessions. Matthew Henry wrote a Scripture catechism, for, said he, "The history of Scripture is most
proper to acquaint your children with in the first place."[2] We
can begin by catechizing little children in the Bible.

LOOKING BACK WE SEE . . . LITTLE CHILDREN

In the dedication of the *Catechism of the Church of Geneva*
John Calvin wrote, "It has ever been the practice of the
Church . . . to see that children should be duly instructed in
the Christian religion."[3] Our survey of history showed that
the Jewish synagogue schools used the catechetical method
of question and answer. Those schools catechized children
from five to ten years of age using the question-and-answer
method and the Old Testament as the only text.

As we've also seen, the early church catechized young
children. A canon attributed to the sixth General Council of
Constantinople (680) promoted schools in all the country
churches. "Very young children were taught to memorize
the Scriptures, and at the same time to understand them."[4]
Later, when the Church of Rome declined, the Waldenses,
Wycliffites, and Bohemian Brethren allowed no child to
grow up without being able to give an account of its faith.[5]

Both the Reformers and the Reformation churches give
evidence that catechism instruction began at an early age.
Calvin insisted children attend catechetical classes. Luther
claimed that "every child under catechetical instruction
ought to know the truths of the entire gospel, . . . by the time
he is nine or ten years of age."[6]

In his *Book of Discipline,* John Knox said, "The young children must be publicly examined in their catechism."[7] One

hundred years after the Reformation began, the churches of Palatinate reported catechism for "boys and girls"; the churches of Emden reported that young children of five and six recited the principal questions of the catechisms.[8] The testimony of the Jewish synagogues, the early church, the forerunners of the Reformation, the Reformers and Reformation churches, and the churches a hundred years later unite in calling for young children to be catechized.

WHO TEACHES?

We've seen that the Scriptures and the confessions are the official possessions of the church, and therefore she is officially responsible for teaching them. That is, catechism must be in the Scriptures and in the confessions because catechism is an official task, and the church through the elders must do three things. First, she must choose a catechism book for Scripture and one for the confessions (see examples in appendix A). Second, she must lay upon parents the responsibility to instruct the children at home in the catechism. Third, she must appoint those who are then to catechize those children. In the next chapters we will discuss those three duties.

Chapter 15

Putting a Program Together

In the previous chapter we determined that the church must officially teach the Scriptures and the confessions in accord with Jesus' command, "As the Father has sent Me, I also send you. Go therefore and make disciples . . . teaching them" (John 20:21; Matt. 28:19–20). In this chapter we'll consider how the elders can do two things: select catechism books and enlist parents.

MEASURING THE MATERIAL

The elders can measure the catechism materials for Bible instruction by two well-defined standards that I call confessional consistency and covenantal unity.

In an earlier chapter we learned that all who teach the Bible do so from a certain perspective. For instance, I teach from a Reformed viewpoint, and that Reformed viewpoint is outlined in the Reformed confessions. Perhaps you teach from another viewpoint, but your teaching should develop from and be consistent with the doctrinal position your church believes is faithful to the Bible as a whole. In applying the first standard, the elders need to assure themselves that the catechism books agree with the confessional position of the church.

We can explain the next standard, covenantal unity, by unfolding the implications of Jesus' statement, "Hear, O Israel, the LORD our God, the LORD is one" (Mark 12:29; Deut. 6:4). Covenantal unity means that although a single thing may have many parts, persons, or aspects, it is yet one harmonious whole. Under this heading we'll examine the covenantal unity (1) of the Trinity, (2) of the Old and New Testaments as the one Word of God, (3) of God and his children, and (4) of the child himself.

UNITY IN TRINITY AND UNITY IN THE WORD

The covenantal unity of God—Father, Son, and Holy Spirit—reveals itself in God's Word and work. The Scriptures are an organic unit: one God, one truth, one salvation, one church, Old Testament and New Testament. The biblical revelation of God, man, and redemption progresses from Genesis to Revelation but is always consistent with the whole.

A small illustration may help us to understand this. A seed of corn looks different from the newly sprouted plant. As the plant grows, more leaves appear; as it reaches six feet, the tassel shoots up. Then the ears begin to form, and the plant's appearance changes at every stage. However, although there is a great difference in appearance and size between the kernel of corn seed and the mature stalk three months later, it is the same plant, and it always was through every stage of development.

The same is true of the living Word of God. Although

Genesis may look different from the Book of Revelation, yet the mature flowering and fruiting of God's great work in the Book of Revelation is the same work whose seed is contained, for example, in Genesis 3:15.

A catechism having covenantal unity avoids presenting Old Testament history as only a series of stories with morals. Although we can gain instruction in character development from the life of Joseph, we miss God's essential purposes in recording the life of Joseph if we see his story as merely one of character development.

When we study Joseph's life, we must see God's plan develop for the redemption of his sinful covenant people, Joseph's brothers. As we read more deeply, we see that redemption not only as a real part of God's unfolding work but also as it leads to Christ. The history of Joseph's plunge, ascent, and reign previews splendidly the redemptive humiliation and exaltation of Christ.

THE UNITY OF GOD AND HIS CHILDREN

"Hear O Israel, the LORD our God, the LORD is one." Covenantal unity presents the Bible as the one Word and work of the one Triune God. But further, the LORD is *our* God. If our catechism material takes seriously covenantal unity, that material will recognize the covenantal unity God created between himself and the children who will learn this material. God has placed these children in a privileged relation to himself in the covenant of grace. The catechism material should impress the children with the precious blessings of covenant keeping and the dire peril of covenant breaking.

Although Moses and all the prophets clearly reveal the glorious promises of God for covenant children, ᵗʰ equally clear that God will visit wrath upon those who despise his Word. The promises *and* warnings of Deuteronomy 28 were written for us and for our children! As the promises are realized in the New Testament in Christ, the warnings are more urgent. "To whom much is given, from him much will be required" (Luke 12:48). The Book of Hebrews continually punctuates its recitation of the surpassing beauty of Christ with predictions of doom and calamity on those who reject him.

THE COVENANTAL UNITY OF THE CHILD

In considering the aspects of covenantal unity, we should address one more. The Scripture catechism material the elders select must speak to the covenantal unity of the child. God created children as prophets, priests, and kings—that is, with intellect, emotion, and will, or, if we state it differently, head, heart, and hands. In presenting the Scriptures the catechism material should give knowledge to the intellect, call for a response of love and faith from the heart, and set before children the necessity of decision and action, the exercise of their will. Anything less is unbalanced.

The standard of covenantal unity looks for an integrated presentation of the one Word and work of God throughout Scripture. We desire that the material will address the child in covenantal unity with God and will call for a covenantally unified response of knowledge, love, and obedience from the child. If I may paraphrase Hebrews 2:3, "How shall our children escape if they neglect so great a salvation?"

Using the standards of confessional consistency and covenantal unity, the elders then can survey the various Bible catechism materials available and make their choice.

In choosing a catechism for the confessions, what standards should the elders use? By his providence God has given the Reformation churches many confessional catechisms. What remains to be found, if needed, are manuals that explain the nature and purpose of confessions, explain the relation of the catechumen to them, and have explanatory notes on the catechisms.

PLACE PARENTS PRIMARY

Having chosen catechism materials, the elders have another essential duty, and that is to set out the role of parents. "Two parties," said Matthew Henry, "parents in their families and . . . ministers in more public assemblies, are necessary, and do mutually assist each other, and neither will excuse the want of the other."[1]

We have to take care that the elders do not usurp the role of parents. In God's covenantal structuring of the church he has never set elders or catechism teachers between parents and children or in place of parents. Elders, therefore, may not shove parents aside, nor may parents vacate their position in favor of elders. Instead, by administering a good catechism program, the elders fulfill their role by insisting and ensuring that the parents of the church obey God's command to instruct their children in his ways (Deut. 6:6–9; Eph. 6:4).

CONFER WITH THE CONGREGATION

The elders would be wise to outline a catechism program and submit it to the congregation for discussion, particularly stressing the role of parents. It is amazing what a little recognition and appreciation of the mind of the congregation will do for the work of elders. And when the program is underway, parents can be invited, even urged, to visit catechism classes occasionally. By doing this parents will show their children, the teacher, the elders, and most importantly, God, that they see the spiritual development of their children to be of major significance.

Another practical point is that fathers, as covenant heads, bear the primary responsibility to make sure children know the catechism lesson. I must say that this truth is more often agreed to in word than in deed. How many of you fathers regularly check your children's catechism? Perhaps you delegate most of the teaching to your wife, but God will call you to give account. "Fathers," says God in Ephesians 6:4, "bring them up in the training and admonition of the Lord." When fathers take an active role, even though it may be limited, the results I have seen are outstanding.

ASSEMBLING THE PARTS

By carefully adopting standards for choosing both Bible and confession catechism material, and by maintaining the biblical roles of father and mother, we as a covenant community can hope to forge a generation of children into a well-tempered sword in the hand of the Lord.

Chapter 16

Catching a Catechist

We come now to the third duty of elders, and that is appointing teachers or catechists who can catechize our children in the Bible and our young people in the confessions. From our previous study we know that teaching the Bible and the confessions is important, for this is an official ministry of the church. We also know that both children and young people are important; yet, some churches teach Bible stories to young children in Sunday school but make certain the pastor teaches doctrine to the teens. Scripture and church history, however, teach us that three groups of men may be assigned as catechists: ministers, elders, and other qualified men.

MINISTERS AS CATECHISTS

It seems that Scripture and church history give priority to ministers of the Word as catechists. We have seen that the ministry of Christ included both preaching and teaching, a pattern the apostles repeated in their work. Paul lists "pastors and teachers" (Eph. 4:11), and he tells Timothy, "a servant of the Lord must [be] . . . able to teach" (2 Tim. 2:24).

Catechizing is part of the minister's calling, a point that

Izerd Van Dellen and Martin Monsma make: "As to catechism work, this certainly belongs to the minister's field of
operation. The teaching of a catechism class is essential ad-
ministration of the Word, just as preaching is."[1] And R. B.
Kuiper, late professor of practical theology at Calvin Seminary, said, "The minister has no more important task than
the education of the covenant youth. Catechetical instruction is on a par with the preaching of the Word."[2]

Reformation and later church history support this view.
John Knox (1505–72) in his *Book of Discipline* said that the
minister must take care of the children and youth, instructing them in the catechism.[3] John Owen (1616–83) said that
next to preaching, catechizing was his most important
work.[4] A contemporary scholar, John J. Murray, quotes Acts
of the Church of England from 1603 and 1639 requiring
every minister to teach catechism.[5] In his sermon on catechism and catechizing, Matthew Henry (1662–1714) says,
"Let the ministers of Christ look upon themselves as under
a charge to feed the lambs of Christ's flock. *All the reformed
churches* make this a part of their [the minister's] work."[6]

ELDERS AS CATECHISTS

The second group of men the elders may appoint as catechists are themselves, for Paul lists being "able to teach" as a
qualification for elders (1 Tim. 3:2). Van Dellen and Monsma
allow that elders may also be appointed, and this could include former or inactive elders. We should recall, however,
that the church when considering elders has historically distinguished between teaching elders, meaning ministers of
the Word, and ruling elders, those having kingly oversight of
the church.

Scripture seems to allow some flexibility in the division of labor between ministers and elders. When elders teach catechism, the church and the elders gain several advantages:

- When an elder teaches catechism, he discovers, as do all teachers, that there is no better way to learn and master material than by teaching it. The elders then become more doctrinally sound and better able to lead the church. In many churches, ministers come and go, but the elders, drawn from among the local congregation, go on. A sound church finds its strength in a sound, able, and doctrinally literate eldership.
- Paul calls elders "shepherds," and catechism teaching is an effective means for a shepherd to know his sheep. Intimate knowledge of family life opens during catechism teaching.
- Elders can continue the work of the ministry of the Word during a vacancy. When the pastor moves, the church may be without a minister for one or more years. Will her responsibility to catechize be neglected? It will not if her elders have played an active role while the pastor was there.

OTHER MEN AS CATECHISTS

The third group from which catechists may be chosen are qualified men from the church. If Paul requires teaching ability in an elder, this must have been demonstrated prior to election to office. Therefore the elders may officially appoint as catechists men who have not held office before. When in the past churches appointed other men, Van Dellen and Monsma note that these catechism teachers "were not appointed before their knowledge, faithfulness, doctrinal purity and piety had been investigated."[7] The Synod of Dort (1618–19) advised that elders observe the teaching of these other men and "show the teachers how they should catechize."[8] We can recall how able ministers of the past marked the difference between lecturing and catechizing, and how very difficult they viewed the task to be.[9]

Setting Priorities, Gaining Blessings

Minister, elders, and other qualified men are the groups that Scripture and church history call to our attention. At the head of these stands the minister, but how is it possible to add teaching six or seven catechism classes to a minister's already busy schedule?

One suggestion is for the elders to examine their minister's duties in the light of the scriptural model (see chap. 6), which places preaching and teaching as primary. If a minister is assigned a host of functions not directly related to teaching and preaching, perhaps it is time to review priorities. Perhaps it is also time for churches to review the duties of the respective offices of elder and minister.

The church of the past regarded catechism teaching as being of primary importance. The elders had, and I suggest they still have, the responsibility to see that the young children and youth are properly catechized in Scripture and the confessions. When elders visit (inspect) each catechism class level at least twice a year, the following blessings result:

- The elders assure themselves and God that they are "guard[ing] what was committed to [their] trust" (1 Tim. 6:20).

- The elders are encouraged that the church will continue in the future on a sound biblical and doctrinal foundation.

- The children, especially the young ones, are impressed that catechism is not a "kid thing" or frivolous entertainment. They know that the church is teaching them the solemn and eternal truths of God, and that they, although they are little children, are of great importance in the kingdom of God.

- The minister or other catechist is greatly stimulated, for the presence of the elders not only convinces him of the importance of catechism but also adds the divine weight of the ruling office to his catechizing. The elder sitting in the corner sharpens the teacher and pricks up the ears of the students.

A POST OF HONOR

This chapter has been devoted to elevating the status of catechism teaching to its ancient rank. The importance of the subject matter (Holy Scripture), the importance of children ("for of such is the kingdom of heaven" [Matt. 19:14]), and an eye of faith to future conquest ("and they overcame him by the blood of the Lamb and by the word of their testimony" [Rev. 12:11]) all press us to appoint skilled and godly men to this great task. The Bible confirms the importance of the man who catechizes; church history solemnly enjoins this ministry upon office bearers; love for Christ compels us to join Peter in listening to our Savior's command, "Feed My lambs!"

Chapter 17

Battle Proven

Americans are a practical people. "Does it work?" they say. "You have a better tractor? Put it in front of this plow, and let's see it in the field." "You developed a better formula for laundry soap? Let's try it and see what happens." We love to make something better, and we won't believe something works until we test it.

It's natural, then, for us to ask, "But does catechism work? Has it been tested? Does teaching by the catechetical formula really produce results?" Our answer to those questions comes from an American, Cotton Mather (1662–1728), who said that if you work hard at catechizing, "you have the experience of all ages to make you hope that vast would be the consequence, vast the advantage."[1]

TRIED AND TRUE

Men and churches have tested teaching Scripture and the confessions by the catechetical method for centuries and have proved it to be powerfully effective. During the Reformation the Roman Catholic Church admitted that the most effective weapon the Protestants used was the exercise of catechizing. In our time John J. Murray attributes the

preservation of Reformation truth and churches in the suc-
ceeding centuries to the catechetical system of instruction.[2]

Catechetical instruction has worked in the past, but will
it work today? Yesterday doesn't count, we are told. The past
has nothing to do with the present. Many people say that
what was true yesterday is not necessarily true today. But we
are Christians, aren't we? God has built our faith and hope
on his unchanging Word. God's commentary on the fallen
nature of man is as true today as when he wrote it. His truth,
grace, mercy, and salvation are the same yesterday, today,
and forever.

Paul faced a hostile world that had its own answers to the
problems of the day. Rome boasted in her legions, her law,
her *pax Romana,* but sin and death still reigned. The Jews
loudly proclaimed that their righteousness was the only answer, but they crucified the Lord of glory. The Greeks said
their wisdom alone held the key, but "they by wisdom knew
not God." When the clamor subsided, sin and death still
reigned. Paul could then assert, "I am not ashamed of the
gospel of Christ, for it is the power of God to salvation for
everyone who believes, for the Jew first and also for the
Greek" (Rom. 1:16). Is it any different today?

DOES CATECHISM PAY DIVIDENDS?

When we think of the word "benefits" we think of
something that does us good. But the first benefit of catechizing is that the name and truth and gospel of Jesus
Christ are honored whenever children memorize, recite,
and sing. The Gospels specially mention the children who
sang psalms to Jesus as he entered Jerusalem on Palm Sunday, and we also read that God has ordained praise from
the mouth of babes.

All benefits received flow from giving. When we give ourselves in obedience to the Lord without thought of personal gain, the promise he made in reference to tithing in Malachi 3:10 becomes ours:

"Prove Me now in this,"
Says the LORD of hosts,
"If I will not open for you the windows of heaven
And pour out for you such blessing
That there will not be room enough to receive it."

In chapter 15 I listed some benefits that elders receive from catechism. The following paragraphs list some benefits to the minister or other catechist and to the church and family. I have heard fathers who turned off the football game and involved themselves in their children's catechism, say, "Boy, do I ever learn a lot from this stuff." So catechism can refresh memories and build up people in the Word.

A GLIMPSE DOWN THE ROAD

When a church looks into the future, forty or fifty years away, does she muse, "Will I still be alive? Or will I be dead like so many others, a shell perhaps, or eviscerated, or embalmed?" If she turns her eyes to the Lord, she will say with Isaiah and Christ, "Behold, I and the children God has given me" (Isa. 8:18; Heb. 2:13). As she catechizes these children in the truth, she may see the church of forty and fifty years later, fit, fighting, and flourishing. The church of tomorrow is her catechized children of today.

I recall a practical expression of this principle. A certain church undertook to build but needed a large loan from the bank. The church's customary bank was reluctant to advance the money without personal guarantees for the whole amount, so the church applied to another bank. That bank had only one request: "Let us see your catechism attendance records." When the bank saw the records the loan was approved. Doesn't it mean something when bankers recognize that faithful catechism teaching is good collateral for a thirty-year loan?

BRINGING IN THE SHEAVES

What promises the Lord gives! We remember that Psalm 127 beautifully confirms that children are a heritage from the Lord. We also know that whether our family has two or twelve children, nurturing them in the fear of the Lord can be a painful exercise. It should not surprise us to see that the last verses of Psalm 126 promise this:

> Those who sow in tears
> Shall reap in joy.
> He who continually goes forth weeping,
> Bearing seed for sowing,
> Shall doubtless come again with rejoicing,
> Bringing his sheaves with him. (vv. 5–6)

The church that catechizes reaps the blessing of God, for God "appointed a law in Israel, which He commanded our fathers, that they should make them known to their children" (Ps. 78:5). "And all these blessings shall come upon you and overtake you because you obeyed the voice of the LORD your God" (Deut. 28:2). We should delight to obey our Savior because we love him. We should catechize our children because he tells us to. How gracious he is to add the promise of blessings to spur us on.

Smoothing Down the Road

Does catechizing benefit the minister? Matthew Henry said, "Catechizing does to the preaching of the Word the same good office that John Baptist did to our Savior; it prepares the way, and makes its paths straight."[3] It does so in multiple ways.

The minister, by teaching small children, learns to present truths in simple ways. He is forced to illustrate by homely examples; he must bring his theological terminology down to talk about spankings and ice-cream cones, seeds and birds, lambs and wolves. As that carries into his preaching, he may find, as I have, that people say, "You know, I can't always follow you because I don't know much, but when you explain something to the children, I can see it plainly."

In many ways the minister gains pastoral insight into the spiritual health of families through catechism. Little children let ministers know what is going on at home. "You don't know your lesson very well this week," observes the minister. "Why?" "Oh," says little Mary, "Mom was too busy to teach me."

Fight to Win

Finally, we look at the world around us. "Behold," said Christ, "I send you out as sheep in the midst of wolves" (Matt. 10:16). Into this world we are going to send our children. Will they survive? More importantly, will they conquer?

Conquest is what our Lord's command is all about. We do not take our children through the training ground of the wilderness merely to leave their bleached bones on the border of Canaan or have them whimper on the banks of Jordan. Instead send them into the land of wickedness, of giants and castles, for "they shall be dust beneath your feet," says the Almighty.

"O brethren," said Richard Baxter, "what a blow we may give the kingdom of darkness by the faithful and skilful managing of this work [catechizing]."[4] John J. Murray, who quoted Baxter in his article on catechizing, concluded, "What a blow was actually given in the days when this Scriptural practice held its place in the Church. And as the true Church of Christ goes forth to battle in our day, as she seeks to storm the strongholds of sin and error, we pray that she may once again be constrained to take up this mighty weapon."[5]

Appendix A

Selected Confessions and Catechisms

Most catechisms find their origin in the confessions of Reformation churches. Some of the confessions still in use are listed below.

CONFESSIONS

CONTINENTAL REFORMED CONFESSIONS

The (Belgic) Confession of Faith. This confession was written in 1561 in what is now Belgium, and it is confessed by many churches today, particularly those of Dutch and German origin. It came into being by way of John Calvin and the French Reformed churches.

Its structure is theological—it confesses the truth about God, man, Christ, salvation, the church, and the last things.

The Heidelberg Catechism. This also is a Continental Reformed confession, adopted in 1563 by the Reformed Churches of the Palatinate (a part of present-day Germany). Along with the Confession of Faith and the Canons of Dort it is confessed by many churches today as one of the Three

Forms of Unity, so called because true unity is found in a common confession of the truth of God's Word.

Its format is catechetical and experiential; that is, it traces by question and answer the manner of God's salvation—bringing the sinner to a consciousness of sin, of deliverance through Christ, and of a life of obedient service and thankfulness.

Canons of Dort. Where the primary aim of the Confession of Faith was a witness to the world, and the focus of the Heidelberg Catechism is believer to believer, the Canons of Dort are addressed primarily to heretics.

The Canons of Dort were formulated by an international synod in the Netherlands city of Dordtrecht meeting from 1618 to 1619. This synod was called by the States-General (government) of the Netherlands to resolve the controversy arising from the teaching of James Arminius, whose followers published his main arguments as the Five Articles of the Remonstrants. That teaching was known from then on as Arminianism and was condemned as heresy by the synod.

The canons are formulated in an apologetic form; that is, under each head of doctrine it first confesses the truth and then rejects errors. The five heads are remembered under the acronym TULIP—total depravity, unconditional election, limited atonement, irresistible grace, and the perseverance of the saints. Historically these have come to be known as the Five Points of Calvinism, although they encompass only a portion of that system of biblical truth reclaimed and taught by John Calvin.

Churches That List Continental Reformed Confessions

What follows is a list of some denominations currently listing these confessions, although not all appear to embrace them with equal tenacity or faithfulness. You can obtain copies of these confessions from them, as well as from some of the bookstores listed in Appendix B.

- American Reformed Churches
- Canadian Reformed Churches
- Christian Reformed Church
- Free Reformed Churches
- Netherlands Reformed Congregations
- Orthodox Christian Reformed Churches
- Protestant Reformed Churches
- Reformed Church in America
- Reformed Church in the U.S.
- United Reformed Churches

PRESBYTERIAN CONFESSIONS

These confessions are as Reformed as are the previous ones. Their origin, however, was in Great Britain rather than on the continent of Europe.

The Westminster Confession. This confession was written in 1647 at Westminster Abbey, London, England, by an assembly of delegates from the churches of Scotland, England, and Ireland. It originated in a time of great Puritan strength, for Oliver Cromwell was on his way to becoming Lord Protector.

This confession, coming as it does about one hundred years after most of the other Reformed confessions, reflects the doctrinal maturity and precision that so many years of struggle, reflection, and study brought. It is arranged in thirty-three chapters, generally following the theological arrangement of the Belgic Confession of Faith.

The Westminster Larger Catechism. This confessional catechism was also written in 1647. It was developed as a practical means to teach the truths of the Westminster Confession. It includes in its coverage, in common with the Heidelberg Catechism and Luther's catechisms, the Apostles' Creed, the Ten Commandments, and the Lord's Prayer.

The Westminster Shorter Catechism. As its name implies, this is an abbreviated version of the Larger Catechism and was formulated at the same time. Its answers are probably more frequently and fondly remembered than those of the Larger since it is primarily used for catechizing children.

Churches That List Presbyterian Confessions

What follows is a list of some denominations currently listing these confessions (again, the reader always does well to determine whether these documents are living confessions or whether the denomination sees them as historical artifacts). You can obtain copies of these confessions from them as well as from some of the bookstores listed in Appendix B.

- American Presbyterian Church
- Associate Reformed Presbyterian Church
- Bible Presbyterian Church (General Synod)
- Evangelical Presbyterian Church
- Free Church of Scotland
- Orthodox Presbyterian Church
- Presbyterian Church (U.S.A.)
- Presbyterian Church in America
- Presbyterian Reformed Church
- Reformed Presbyterian Church (General Assembly)
- Reformed Presbyterian Church of North America

REFORMED BAPTIST CONFESSIONS

The Reformed Baptists, as their name implies, blend two Reformation streams. Poh Boon Sing, in a booklet entitled *What Is a Reformed Baptist Church,* says that they originated from both the Magisterial Reformation, represented by the Lutheran, Calvinist, and Zwinglian sections, and from the Radical Reformation, represented by the evangelical Anabaptists. C. H. Spurgeon was a Reformed Baptist.

Reformed Baptists are particularly distinguished from Reformed and Presbyterian churches in that the former hold to believer's baptism by immersion and deny infant baptism.

The London Baptist Confession of Faith of 1689. This confession is based on the Westminster Confession, and in most chapters it is identical. The chief differences with the Westminster Confession lie, as expected, in the doctrines of the church and baptism.

The Philadelphia Confession of Faith of 1742. This is the London Confession as adopted by the Baptist Association in 1742 at Philadelphia.

Churches That List Reformed Baptist Confessions

Reformed Baptist Churches. This is not a denomination, since very few Reformed Baptist Churches have formed any sort of denominational structure. They generally continue as independent, yet they often enjoy a good measure of association with one another. They usually but not always carry the term "Reformed Baptist" in their congregational name.

UNITY OF FAITH

Perhaps it's good to realize at this point that although we've covered eight different confessions and listed quite a few churches or denominations, golden threads of common biblical truth not only bind the confessions together but also unite all those churches that confess these truths with faithfulness.

If you think eight confessions are quite a few, John H. Leith noted in *Creeds of the Churches,* "More than sixty creeds would qualify as Reformed."[1] Yet their basic unity was expressed so well by Henry Bullinger and Leo Judae, who were said to have added this comment to their signature on the First Helvetic Confession (Switzerland, 1536):

> We wish in no way to prescribe for all churches through these articles a single rule of faith. For we acknowledge no other rule of faith than Holy Scripture. We agree with whoever agrees with this, although he uses different expressions from our Confession. For we should have regard for the fact itself and for the truth, not for the words. We grant to everyone the freedom to use his own expressions which are suitable for his church and will make use of this freedom ourselves, at the same time defending the true sense of this Confession against distortions.[2]

CATECHISMS

The sources for both Scripture and confession catechisms will be listed after each. Addresses will be found at the end of the list. Many of those available at the bookstores listed can be ordered from your own bookstore as well.

It does not appear possible to make an exhaustive list. While I have attempted to list only worthy catechisms, my judgment is necessarily limited and subjective. You are urged to examine catechisms thoroughly before using them.

If you have read this book, you will understand that I believe catechizing in the Bible should come before catechizing in doctrine or confessions. So this list will begin with Scripture catechisms and then go on to confession catechisms.

SCRIPTURE CATECHISMS

Many Sunday school curricula seem to be designed for this area, but most show a lack of cohesiveness and thematic unity. They seem to present a series of interesting biblical stories that are loosely connected by historical sequence and vaguely designed to instill worthy values and good morals.

It does seem strange when the level of biblical knowledge among many professing Christians is plunging toward zero that there should be such a dearth of Scripture catechisms. Matthew Henry said that this is the natural and essential starting point for catechetical instruction. Young children should be catechized first in the Scriptures.

I pray and trust that there are more Scripture catechisms than I have been able to locate.

To You Is the Promise and to Your Children, **Harry Van Dyken**

Description: This series of six books covers the entire Bible as the redemptive, covenantal revelation of God. The books are written from a Continental Reformed perspective and stress the glory and meaning of the covenant.

Book 1—For Beginners covers Genesis to Malachi. Memory questions and answers, memory song, and text. 25 lessons, 99 pages. Ages 5–7.

Book 2—Genesis to II Samuel. Memory questions and answers, memory song, and text. Lesson and knowledge questions. 25 lessons, 108 pages. Ages 6–8.

Book 3—I Kings to Malachi. Memory questions and answers, memory song, and text. Lesson and knowledge questions. 25 lessons, quarterly tests, 125 pages. Ages 7–9.

Book 4—The Gospels. Memory questions and answers, memory song, and text. Lesson and knowledge questions. 25 lessons, quarterly tests, 123 pages. Ages 8–10.

Book 5—The Acts. Memory questions and answers. Lesson and knowledge questions. 25 lessons, quarterly tests, 117 pages. Ages 9–12.

Book 6—The Epistles and Revelation. Memory questions and answers. Lesson and knowledge questions. 25 lessons, quarterly tests, 109 pages. Ages 11–13.

Publisher: Line of Promise Press
Bookstores: Line of Promise Press, Speelman's Bookhouse Ltd. (Canada).

Old Testament Bible Stories—Book I, Cornelius Hanko

Description: From Creation to Saul. Questions and answers. 25 lessons, 28 pages. Grades 1–3.
Publisher: Protestant Reformed Churches in America
Bookstores: Catechism Book Committee, Protestant Reformed Seminary

Old Testament Bible Stories—Book II, Cornelius Hanko

Description: From Saul to the Return from Captivity. Questions and answers. 25 lessons, 28 pages. Grades 1–3.
Publisher: Protestant Reformed Churches in America

Bookstores: Catechism Book Committee, Protestant Reformed Seminary

New Testament Bible Stories—Book III, Cornelius Hanko

Description: Questions and answers. 25 lessons, 28 pages. Grades 1–3.

Publisher: Protestant Reformed Churches in America

Bookstores: Catechism Book Committee, Protestant Reformed Seminary

Bible History Presented in Questions and Answers for Beginners, P. Dyksterhuis

Description: Covers Old and New Testaments. Questions and answers only. 42 lessons, 45 pages.

Publisher: Netherlands Reformed Book and Publishing

Bookstores: Publisher, Reformation Heritage Books

Short Questions for Little Children, Jacobus Borstius

Description: Bible history and doctrine. Questions and answers only. 28 lessons, 32 pages.

Publisher: Netherlands Reformed Book and Publishing

Bookstores: Publisher, Reformation Heritage Books

Old Testament History in Brief, H. C. Hoeksema

Description: Questions and answers. 25 lessons, 28 pages. Workbook, 25 lessons, 50 pages. Grades 4 and 5.

Publisher: Protestant Reformed Churches in America

Bookstores: Catechism Book Committee, Protestant Reformed Seminary

Old Testament History, G. Vanden Berg

Description: Workbook. 25 lessons, 50 pages. Grades 4 and 5.

Publisher: Protestant Reformed Churches in America

Bookstores: Catechism Book Committee, Protestant Reformed Seminary

New Testament History, G. Vanden Berg

Description: Questions and answers. 25 lessons, 28 pages. Workbook, 25 lessons, 50 pages. Grades 4 and 5.

Publisher: Protestant Reformed Churches in America

Bookstores: Catechism Book Committee, Protestant Reformed Seminary

Old Testament History for Seniors, John A. Heys

Description: Questions and answers. 25 lessons, 28 pages. Workbook, 25 lessons, 50 pages. Grades 6 and 7.

Publisher: Protestant Reformed Churches in America

Bookstores: Catechism Book Committee, Protestant Reformed Seminary

New Testament History for Seniors, Herman Veldman

Description: Questions and answers. 25 lessons, 28 pages. Workbook, 25 lessons, 50 pages. Grades 6 and 7.

Publisher: Protestant Reformed Churches in America

Bookstores: Catechism Book Committee, Protestant Reformed Seminary

CONFESSION CATECHISMS

The Heidelberg Catechism—A Study Guide, G. I. Williamson

Description: A guide to the study of the Heidelberg Catechism. 241 pages. Designed for the catechetical instruction of youth.

Publisher: P&R Publishing

Bookstores: Cumberland Valley Bible Book Store or local bookstore.

Study Helps on the Heidelberg Catechism, Norman L. Jones

Description: Title describes contents. Commentary and review questions. Reformed Church U.S. 129 lessons, glossary, 290 pages.

Publisher: Publications Committee, Reformed Church in the U.S.

Bookstores: Book Depository, Reformed Church in the U.S.

I Belong—A Course of Study on the Heidelberg Catechism, James Visscher

Description: Title describes contents. Student workbooks: volume 1, 224 pages; volume 2, 240 pages. Teacher's manual, 168 pages. Canadian Reformed.

Publisher: Premier Publishing

Bookstores: Publisher, Speelman's Bookhouse Ltd. (Canada), or local bookstore.

Before the Face of God, Louis Praamsma

Description: A study of the Heidelberg Catechism in two workbooks for catechism students; volume 1, Lord's Days 1–24, 100 pages; volume 2, Lord's Days 25–52, 117 pages.

Publisher: Inheritance Publications

Bookstores: Inheritance Publications

Heidelberg Catechism

Description: Two memory books, each 26 Lord's days, 28 lessons, 56 pages, by Wilbur Bruinsma. Two workbooks, each 26 Lord's days, 28 lessons, 52 pages, by Dale H. Kuiper.

Publisher: Protestant Reformed Churches in America

Bookstores: Catechism Book Committee, Protestant Reformed Seminary

Simple Instructions in Bible Truths for Catechising, J. H. Donner

Description: Doctrinal. Only questions and answers. 22 lessons, 31 pages.

Publisher: Netherlands Reformed Book and Publishing
Bookstores: Publisher, Reformation Heritage Books

Simple Catechism Questions for Children, L. G. C. Ledeboer

Description: Doctrinal. Only questions and answers. 1 lesson, 97 questions, 12 pages.

Publisher: Netherlands Reformed Book and Publishing
Bookstores: Publisher, Reformation Heritage Books

First Book of Christian Doctrine, by G. W. Hylkema and E. J. Tuuk

Description: Traditional questions and answers, etc. Grades 3 and 4. Christian Reformed, 145 pages.

Publisher: Reformed Fellowship Inc.
Bookstores: Reformed Fellowship Inc.

An Introduction to the Compendium of Reformed Doctrine, Y. P. De Jong (revised by A. C. De Jong and J. H. Piersma)

Description: "A catechism for junior high students containing questions and answers, written work assignments, lesson explanations and biblical word studies." 25 lessons, 53 pages. Christian Reformed.

Publisher: Reformed Fellowship Inc.
Bookstores: Reformed Fellowship Inc.

Essentials of Reformed Doctrine, H. Hoeksema

Description: Question and answer. 30 lessons, 66 pages. High school.

Publisher: Protestant Reformed Churches in America

Bookstores: Catechism Book Committee, Protestant Reformed Seminary

A Specimen of Divine Truths for Those Who Are Preparing for Confession of Faith, Abraham Hellenbroek

Description: Doctrinal. Question and answer. 21 chapters, 85 pages.

Publisher: Netherlands Reformed Book and Publishing

Bookstores: Publisher, Reformation Heritage Books

Doctrinal Review, H. Hoeksema

Description: Question and answer. 12 pages.

Publisher: Protestant Reformed Churches in America

Bookstores: Catechism Book Committee, Protestant Reformed Seminary

Learning to Know the Lord, P. Y. De Jong

Description: Studies in Reformed doctrine for high school catechumens. Christian Reformed. 28 lessons, 63 pages.

Publisher: Reformed Fellowship Inc.

Bookstores: Reformed Fellowship Inc.

Compendium of the Christian Religion

Description: Questions and answers with Scripture texts only. No lesson material. Based on the Heidelberg Catechism and formulated by the CRC Committee on Education in 1957. 42 lessons, 64 pages.

Publisher: CRC Publications

Bookstores: CRC Publications

A Treatise of the Compendium, **G. H. Kersten**

Description: The compendium is an abridgment of the Heidelberg Catechism. This book accompanies it with explanations. Workbooks accompanying this study guide are also available. 142 pages.

Publisher: Netherlands Reformed Book and Publishing Committee

Bookstores: Gospel Mission; Netherlands Reformed Book and Publishing Committee.

Everything in Christ, **Clarence Stam**

Description: Catechetical instruction in the Belgic Confession. Includes outlines on church history, polity, and liturgy. 174 pages. Canadian Reformed.

Publisher: Premier Publishing

Bookstores: Publisher, Speelman's Bookhouse Ltd. (Canada), or local bookstore.

But for the Grace of God, **Cornelis P. Venema**

Description: An exposition of the Canons of Dort (TULIP—five points of Calvinism). 145 pages.

Publisher: Reformed Fellowship Inc.

Bookstores: Reformed Fellowship Inc.

Unspeakable Comfort: A Commentary on the Canons of Dort, **Peter G. Feenstra**

Description: Title describes. Explanation of TULIP (five points of Calvinism). 210 pages. Canadian Reformed.

Publisher: Premier Publishing

Bookstores: Publisher, Speelman's Bookhouse Ltd. (Canada), or local bookstore.

The Five Points of Calvinism—Defined, Defended, Documented, **David N. Steele and Curtis C. Thomas**

Description: This is a study manual rather than a question-and-answer catechism. It can be taught by the catechetical method. The title describes its contents. The five points of Calvinism are total depravity, unconditional election, limited atonement, irresistible grace, and perseverance of the saints. 95 pages.

Publisher: P&R Publishing
Bookstores: Cumberland Valley Bible Book Service, Crown & Covenant Publications

What We Believe, Cornelis P. Venema

Description: An exposition of the Apostles' Creed. 136 pages.
Publisher: Reformed Fellowship Inc.
Bookstores: Reformed Fellowship Inc.

A Summary of Christian Doctrine, Louis Berkhof

Description: Follows the six loci of theology: the doctrines of God, man, Christ, salvation, the church, and the last things. Explanation, scripture memory, Scripture study, questions for review. For advanced catechetical instruction. 30 lessons, 184 pages.

Publisher: Banner of Truth Trust
Bookstores: Cumberland Valley Bible Book Service

The Shorter Catechism—For Study Classes, 2 volumes, G. I. Williamson

Description: A guide to the study of the Westminster Shorter Catechism. Volume 1, 170 pages; volume 2, 175 pages. Presbyterian.

Publisher: P&R Publishing
Bookstores: Cumberland Valley Bible Book Service, Covenant Home Curriculum, Speelman's Bookhouse Ltd. (Canada), or local bookstore

Complete Shorter Catechism

Description: Presbyterian. A complete teaching package, including

1. The Shorter Catechism with Scripture Proofs booklet.
2. *The Shorter Catechism—For Study Classes,* volumes 1 and 2 (described above), G. I. Williamson, with quarterly tests. 170 and 165 pages.
3. *The Concise Survey of the Westminster Shorter Catechism* (study guide with key), Dale K. Dykema. 76 pages.
4. Day-by-day scheduling guides for each module.

Publisher: 1—Banner of Truth, 2—P&R Publishing, 3 and 4—Covenant Home Curriculum

Bookstores: Covenant Home Curriculum

The Shorter Catechism Explained from Scripture, **Thomas Vincent**

Description: An exposition of the Westminster Shorter Catechism. 282 pages.

Publisher: Banner of Truth

Bookstores: Cumberland Valley Bible Book Service or local bookstore.

Training Hearts, Teaching Minds: Family Devotions Based on the Shorter Catechism, **Starr Meade**

Description: A simple guide to the Westminster Shorter Catechism with a week's worth of brief daily readings on each question. 353 pages. Designed to assist memorization and comprehension by the whole family.

Publisher: P&R Publishing

Bookstores: Publisher or local bookstore

Westminster Shorter Catechism Memory Cards

Description: Each card has a catechism question on one side and the answer on the back. 107 cards with container.

Publisher: Great Commission Publications

Bookstores: Great Commission Publications, Crown & Covenant Publications

Understanding Biblical Doctrine, Ronald W. Nickerson

Description: Workbook format covering basic Reformed doctrine. 70 pages. Junior high through adult. Leader's guide also available. 44 pages. Reformed Presbyterian.

Publisher: Crown & Covenant Publications

Bookstores: Crown & Covenant Publications

Big Truths for Little Kids, Susan and Richie Hunt

Description: Includes questions and answers from children's catechisms, short stories to illustrate truths. 160 pages.

Publisher: Crossway

Bookstores: Cumberland Valley Bible Book Service

The Big Book of Questions and Answers: A Family Guide to the Christian Faith, Sinclair B. Ferguson

Description: 77 simple questions and answers, each with a memory verse, related activities, and prayer. 95 pages.

Publisher: Christian Focus

Bookstores: Publisher or local bookstore

Things Most Surely Believed Among Us, W. Gadsby

Description: A doctrinal catechism for children containing 109 questions and answers. 24 pages. Reformed Baptist.

Publisher: Gospel Standard Publications (England—Gospel Standard Strict Baptists)

Bookstores: Gospel Mission

Catechism with Proofs, C. H. Spurgeon

Description: Based on the Westminster and Baptist Catechisms for children. 32 pages. Reformed Baptist.

Publisher: Chapel Library

Bookstores: Gospel Mission, Trinity Book Service

Appendix B

Publishers and Bookstores

Banner of Truth
> P. O. Box 621
> Carlisle, PA 17013
> Phone: 717-249-5747
> Fax: 717-249-0604
> E-mail: jbebanneroftruth@compuserve.com
> Web site: www.banneroftruth.co.uk

Catechism Book Committee
> Protestant Reformed Seminary
> 4949 Ivanrest Avenue
> Grandville, MI 49418
> Phone: 616-531-1490
> E-mail: 74170.3215@compuserve.com

Chapel Library
> 2603 W. Wright Street
> Pensacola, FL 32505
> Phone: 850-438-6666

Covenant Home Curriculum
   W23421 Main Street
   Sussex, WI 53089
   Phone: 800-578-2421
   Fax: 262-246-7066
   E-mail: dkdykema@covenanthome.com
   Web site: www.covenanthome.com

CRC Publications
   2850 Kalamazoo Avenue, S.E.
   Grand Rapids, MI 49560
   Phone: 800-333-8300

Crown & Covenant Publications (RPCNA)
   7408 Penn Avenue
   Pittsburgh, PA 15208-2531
   Phone: 412-241-0436
   Fax: 412-731-8861
   E-mail: psalms4u@aol.com
   Web site: www.psalms4u.com

Cumberland Valley Bible Book Service
   P. O. Box 613
   Carlisle, PA 17013
   Phone: 717-249-0231
   Credit card order: 800-656-0231
   Fax: 717-243-5490
   E-mail: cvbbs@cvbbs.com
   Web site: www.cvbbs.com

Gospel Mission
   P. O. Box 318
   Choteau, MT 59422
   Phone and fax: 406-466-2311

Great Commission Publications
    3640 Windsor Park Drive
    Suwanee, GA 30024-3897
    Phone: 800-695-3387
    Fax (770) 271-5657
    Web site: www.gcp.org

Inheritance Publications
    Box 154
    Neerlandia, AB CANADA T0G 1R0
    Phone and fax: 780-674-3949
    E-mail: inhpubl@telusplanet.net
    Web site:
    www.telusplanet.net/public/inhpubl/webip/ip.htm

Line of Promise Press
    P. O. Box 1242
    Sunnyside, WA 98944
    Phone: 509-837-2229
    Fax: 509-837-2292
    E-mail: vandyken@bentonrea.com

Netherlands Reformed Book and Publishing Committee
    1233 Leffingwell, N.E.
    Grand Rapids, MI 49525

Premier Printing Ltd.
    One Beghin Avenue
    Winnipeg, MB CANADA R2J 3X5
    Phone: 204-663-9000
    Fax: 204-663-9202

P&R Publishing
Presbyterian and Reformed Publishing Company
    P. O. Box 817
    Phillipsburg, NJ 08865-0817
    Phone: 908-454-0505
    Fax: 908-859-2390
    Web site: www.prpbooks.com

Reformation Heritage Books
    2919 Leonard Street, N.E.
    Grand Rapids, MI 49525
    Phone: 616-977-0599 or 616-977-0833
    Fax: 616-977-0889 or 616-285-3246
    E-mail: rhb-inc@wybbs.mi.org or jrbeeke@aol.com
    Web site: www.heritagebooks.org

Reformed Church in the U.S.
    Book Depository
    c/o Dave McPherson
    1303 Evergreen Drive
    Sturgis, SD 57785
    Phone: 605-347-5666
    Fax: 605-347-2788

Reformed Fellowship, Inc.
    2930 Chicago Drive, S.W.
    Grandville, MI 49418
    616-532-8510

Speelman's Bookhouse Ltd.
    5010 Steeles Avenue W., Unit # 12
    Rexdale, ON CANADA M9V 5C6
    Phone: 416-741-6563
    Fax: 416-748-3062

Trinity Book Service
  P. O. Box 569
  Montville, NJ 07045
  Phone: 800-722-3584
  Fax: 973-402-2688
  E-mail: TrntyBkSvc@aol.com
  Web site:
  http://store.yahoo.com/trinitybookservice/

Notes

Chapter 1: A Tale of Two Cities

1 John Calvin, *Catechism of the Church of Geneva* (Edinburgh: Calvin Translation Society, 1849), 36.

Chapter 2: Anchoring in the Past

1 John J. Murray, "Catechizing—A Forgotten Practice," *Banner of Truth* 27 (October 1962), 15, emphasis added.

2 Quoted by H. Clay Trumbull, *The Sunday-School* (Philadelphia: John D. Wattles, 1893), 73.

3 The Reverend Ronald C. Christie, "Teaching Face to Face," *The Monthly Record*, Scotland (reprinted in the Associate Reformed Presbyterian quarterly *The Highroad* 16, no. 1 [spring 1994]: 7).

4 John Calvin, *Catechism of the Church of Geneva* (Edinburgh: Calvin Translation Society, 1849), 37.

Chapter 3: The Meaning of Catechizing

1 Craig R. Thompson, "Introduction" to Desiderius Erasmus, *Ten Colloquies* (Indianapolis: Liberal Arts Press, 1957), xxiii–xxiv.

2 For an illustration of teaching by question and answer, turn to chapter 10.

Chapter 4: The Meaning and Place of Catechisms

1 Matthew Henry, "The Catechizing of Youth," a sermon from *The Complete Works of Matthew Henry*, 2 vols. (Edinburgh: Fullarton & Co., 1855), 2:160–61.

2 G. I. Williamson, *The Shorter Catechism, for Study Classes*, 2 vols. (Phillipsburg, N.J.: Presbyterian and Reformed, 1970); G. I. Williamson, *The Heidelberg Catechism—A Study Guide* (Phillipsburg, N.J.: Presbyterian and Reformed, 1993).

3 Williamson, *The Heidelberg Catechism—A Study Guide*, 2, 3.

Chapter 5: The Importance of Catechism

1 John J. Murray, "Catechizing—A Forgotten Practice," *Banner of Truth* 27 (October 1962), 18.

2 Translator's preface in John Calvin, *Catechism of the Church of Geneva* (Edinburgh: Calvin Translation Society, 1849), xi.

3 Two examples of God's promises for our children are "And the LORD your God will circumcise your heart and the heart of your descendants, to love the LORD your God with all your heart and with all your soul, that you may live" (Deut. 30:6) and "All your children shall be taught by the LORD, and great shall be the peace of your children" (Isa. 54:13).

4 Murray, "Catechizing—A Forgotten Practice," 26.

5 Ibid.

6 Clarence H. Benson, *History of Christian Education* (Chicago: Moody Press, 1943), 46. There is nothing new under the sun, is there?

7 From the preface to the catechism of the Council of Trent, question vi, quoted by H. Clay Trumbull, *The Sunday-School* (Philadelphia: John D. Wattles, 1893), 95.

8 Quoted in Trumbull, *The Sunday-School,* 73.

9 Cited in ibid., 70.

10 Francis Xavier, one of the founders of the Jesuits, is reputed to have said, "Give me the children until they are seven years old, and anyone may take them afterwards." Cited in ibid., 71.

11 Izerd Van Dellen and Martin Monsma, *The Church Order Commentary* (Grand Rapids: Zondervan, 1949), 256.

12 William Shedd, *Pastoral Theology* (New York: Charles Scribner, 1867), 407.

13 Ibid. 429.

Chapter 6: The History of Catechizing: Moses to Paul

1 Deut. 18:5.

2 Josh. 21.

3 Deut. 12:18.

4 Deut. 33:10; Mal. 2:7.

5 Clarence H. Benson, *History of Christian Education* (Chicago: Moody Press, 1943), 8.

6 Ibid., 28.

7 Ibid.

8 Ibid., 29.

Notes

....

Chapter 7: The History of Catechizing: Alexandria to Massachusetts

1 Clarence H. Benson, *History of Christian Education* (Chicago: Moody Press, 1943), 42.

2 August Dorner, "Augustinus," in *Schaff-Herzog Encyclopaedia of Religious Knowledge*, ed. Philip Schaff, 4 vols. (New York: Funk & Wagnalls, 1894), 1:174.

3 *Bingham's Antiquities*, bk. xiii, chap. 7, cited by H. Clay Trumbull, *The Sunday-School* (Philadelphia: John D. Wattles, 1893), 62.

4 Kenneth Scott Latourette, *A History of Christianity* (New York: Harper & Row, 1975), 357.

5 "Catechetics, Catechisms, and Catechumens," in *Schaff-Herzog Encyclopaedia of Religious Knowledge*, 1:417–19.

6 K. Dijk, "Catechesis," in *Christelijke Encyclopedie*, (Kampen: J. H. Kok, 1956), 116–17, trans. N. Gazendam.

7 Translator's preface to John Calvin, *Catechism of the Church of Geneva* (Edinburgh: Calvin Translation Society, 1849), xi.

8 Benson, *History of Christian Education*, 82.

9 Cited in ibid., 77.

10 Ibid., 83.

11 Trumbull, *The Sunday-School*, 74.

12 All of the information about the synod's discussion of catechism is from L. H. Wagenaar, *Van Strijd en Overwinning* [*Of Battle and Victory*] (Utrecht: G. J. A. Ruys, 1909), 335–38.

13 Benson, *History of Christian Education*, 107. The Heidelberg Catechism has the distinction of being the first Protestant catechism used in America. Hendrick Hudson, the explorer of the Hudson River and Hudson Bay, brought it from Holland to Manhattan Island in 1609. See Philip Schaff, *The Creeds of Christendom*, 3 vols. (reprint; Grand Rapids: Baker, 1983), 1:549.

Chapter 8: An Encouraging Word

1 I have known a number of immigrants from the Netherlands who, having been catechized in their youth, still remembered the psalms they had learned to sing sixty years earlier.

Thomas Carlyle (1795–1881), Scottish historian and social critic, was brought up in a typical Scottish Calvinist family. Toward the end of his life he said, "The older I grow—and I now stand upon the brink of eternity—the more comes back to me the first sentence in the

[Westminster Shorter] Catechism, which I learned when a child, and the fuller and deeper its meaning becomes: 'What is the chief end of man?—To glorify God and to enjoy him forever.' " Cited by Alexander F. Mitchell in *Catechisms of the Second Reformation* (London: James Nisbet & Co., 1886), xxxvii–xxxviii.

2 For the Reformation explanation and defense of infant baptism I recommend the following books: Kenneth L. Gentry Jr., *Infant Baptism, a Duty of God's People* (Christian Education Committee, Westminster Presbytery, Presbyterian Church in America, 1988); Jim West, *The Covenant Baptism of Infants* (Christian Worldview Ministries, P. O. Box 603, Palo Cedro, CA 96073-0603, 1994); H. Westerink, *A Sign of Faithfulness, Covenant and Baptism* (Inheritance Publications, Box 154, Neerlandia, AB, Canada TOG 1RO, 1997); Douglas Wilson, *To a Thousand Generations: Infant Baptism, Covenant Mercy for the People of God* (Canon Press, P. O. Box 8741, Moscow, ID 83843, 1996); and Robert R. Booth, *Children of the Promise: The Biblical Case for Infant Baptism* (Phillipsburg, N.J.: Presbyterian and Reformed, 1995). Both Robert R. Booth and Douglas Wilson are former Baptists whom the Scriptures brought to embrace infant baptism.

Another source is Pierre Ch. Marcel, *The Biblical Doctrine of Infant Baptism, Sacrament of the Covenant of Grace* (London: James Clarke & Co. Ltd., 1953). This work was originally published in French in 1951 and then translated by the Reverend Philip E. Hughes. Marcel writes with great breadth and depth and with a spirit of charity. In the foreword he states, "My desire is that this study should be read and used in the same spirit as that in which I have wished to write it. I should be distressed were certain people to handle it without love as a weapon of battle to reduce the 'adversary' to silence." For a scholarly and comprehensive approach, this book is the best.

Hughes Oliphant Old, *The Shaping of the Reformed Baptismal Rite in the Sixteenth Century* (Grand Rapids: Eerdmans, 1992) is especially helpful for understanding the origins of the Anabaptist movement and its spiritual heirs, the Baptists. Old brings exhaustive research to show how the rejection of infant baptism began during the Reformation and how the Reformers responded by more clearly articulating that doctrine.

3 Baptism saves no one; Jesus alone saves. Baptism is a sign and seal not of my action, but of God's. It identifies and authenticates a reality greater than itself, greater than I, and greater than the baby.

Notes

Chapter 9: Covenantal Catechism

1 The concept of confessions was introduced in chapter 4.

2 One of the sad facts of family life today is that parents and particularly mothers drop off their little children at day-care centers. When the children are teenagers and older, Mom is dismayed to find they are strangers. But doesn't the church as a mother do the same thing when she sends her children out of the worship service into a kind of ecclesiastical day-care center, children's church? Should she wonder, then, that when her children grow older they are strangers to Christ?

3 The Heidelberg Catechism is also a confession of many churches today, particularly those of German and Dutch origin. It is a Reformation confession in the form of questions and answers, adopted in 1563 in Heidelberg, Germany. Its pattern follows that of the Old Testament history of Israel from Egypt to Sinai, and the New Testament Book of Romans. It deals first with our sinful state of slavery, then with our great deliverance through Christ, and finally with the manner in which we may express our love and thankfulness to God for this great salvation, namely, by obedience to his laws.

4 Some children of the covenant refuse to respond in faith and obedience, but they reap and will reap the curse. We do not, however, catechize on the assumption that they will spiritually die, any more than when a baby is born, we love, nourish, and care for it with the assumption that it will die before maturity. There are times, in the infinite wisdom and providence of God, that babies die in infancy despite all the care and love lavished on them. Likewise there are times, in the infinite wisdom and providence of God, that children of the covenant break that covenant, fail to come to spiritual life in Christ, and come under the sentence of eternal death despite all the spiritual care and love lavished upon them.

We must place our faith in Christ. There is no basis for confidence in our greatest efforts in faithful child rearing or in the church but only in the Word and promise of Christ. He said, "Let the little children come to Me, and do not forbid them," and "I have come that they may have life, and that they may have it more abundantly" (Luke 18:16; John 10:10).

Chapter 10: How Shall We Teach Catechism?

1 John Henry Newman in "What Is a University?" *Harvard Classics*, 51 vols. (New York: P. F. Collier, 1938), 28:37–38.

2 H. Clay Trumbull, *The Sunday-School* (Philadelphia: John D. Wattles, 1893), 88.

3 Cited in John J. Murray, "Catechizing—A Forgotten Practice," *Banner of Truth* 27 (October 1962), 20.

4 Murray, "Catechizing—A Forgotten Practice," 20.

5 Cited in ibid.

Chapter 11: Teaching Catechism: Memorizing and Questioning

1 1 Cor. 9:19–22.

2 Ps. 104:30.

3 L. H. Wagenaar, *Van Strijd en Overwinning* [*Of Battle and Victory*] (Utrecht: G. J. A. Ruys, 1909), 336.

4 Matthew Henry, "The Catechizing of Youth," a sermon from *The Complete Works of Matthew Henry*, 2 vols. (Edinburgh: Fullarton & Co., 1855), 2:166.

5 John Jebb, *Pastoral Instructions*, 198, quoted in H. Clay Trumbull, *The Sunday-School* (Philadelphia: John D. Wattles, 1893), 80.

Chapter 12: Teaching Catechism: Review and Repetition

1 Cited in Clarence H. Benson, *History of Christian Education* (Chicago: Moody Press, 1943), 28.

2 In its sublime simplicity the first question and answer read: What is your only comfort in life and death?

> *That I, with body and soul, both in life and death, am not my own, but belong unto my faithful Savior Jesus Christ; who with his precious blood has fully satisfied for all my sins, and delivered me from all the power of the devil; and so preserves me that without the will of my heavenly Father not a hair can fall from my head; yea, that all things must be subservient to my salvation, wherefore by his Holy Spirit he also assures me of eternal life, and makes me heartily willing and ready, henceforth, to live unto him.*

3 William Hendriksen, *Survey of the Bible* (Grand Rapids: Baker, 1978).

Chapter 13: Teaching Catechism: Learning and Singing Songs

1 The whole story of Jean Cavalier and others, is told by Henry Charles Moore, *Through Flood and Flame: Adventures and Perils of Protestant Heroes* (East Sussex, England: Focus Christian Ministries Trust, n.d.).

2 *Psalter Hymnal* (Grand Rapids: Publication Committee of the Christian Reformed Church, Inc., 1959), no. 124, verse 1, from Ps. 68.

Notes

3 Ibid, no. 442, verse 3.

4 Jan Smelik, "Theology and Music," *Diakonia* 7, no. 2 (December 1993): 45.

5 Harry Van Dyken, *To You Is the Promise and to Your Children, Book 3* (Sunnyside, Wash.: Line of Promise Press, 1991), 5.

6 Zillah is a town in the Yakima Valley of Washington State.

7 *Psalter Hymnal* (Grand Rapids: Publication Committee of the Christian Reformed Church, Inc., 1959), no. 237, verse 1, from Ps. 119.

8 Ibid., no. 205, verse 3, from Ps. 103.

9 Ibid., no. 190, verse 1, from Ps. 98.

10 Ibid., no. 122, verse 1, from Ps. 68.

Chapter 14: Who Is Taught? Who Teaches?

1 H. Clay Trumbull, *The Sunday-School* (Philadelphia: John D. Wattles, 1893), 70.

2 Matthew Henry, "The Catechizing of Youth," a sermon from *The Complete Works of Matthew Henry,* 2 vols. (Edinburgh: Fullarton & Co., 1855), 2:170.

3 John Calvin, *Catechism of the Church of Geneva* (Edinburgh: Calvin Translation Society, 1849).

4 Trumbull, *The Sunday-School,* 63.

5 "Catechetics, Catechisms, and Catechumens," in *Schaff-Herzog Encyclopaedia of Religious Knowledge,* ed. Philip Schaff, 4 vols. (New York: Funk & Wagnalls, 1894), 1:418.

6 Cited in Trumbull, *The Sunday-School,* 77.

7 Cited in Clarence H. Benson, *History of Christian Education* (Chicago: Moody Press, 1943), 83.

8 L. H. Wagenaar, *Van Strijd en Overwinning* [*Of Battle and Victory*] (Utrecht: G. J. A. Ruys, 1909), 336.

Chapter 15: Putting a Program Together

1 Matthew Henry, "The Catechizing of Youth," a sermon from *The Complete Works of Matthew Henry,* 2 vols. (Edinburgh: Fullarton & Co., 1855), 2:157.

Chapter 16: Catching a Catechist

1 Izerd Van Dellen and Martin Monsma, *The Church Order Commentary* (Grand Rapids: Zondervan, 1949), 75.

2 R. B. Kuiper, "Catechetics," unpublished class notes, Calvin Theological Seminary, c. 1953.

3 Clarence H. Benson, *History of Christian Education* (Chicago: Moody Press, 1943), 83.

4 John Owen, cited in John J. Murray, "Catechizing—A Forgotten Practice," *Banner of Truth* 27 (October 1962), 18.

5 Murray, "Catechizing—A Forgotten Practice," 17.

6 Matthew Henry, "The Catechizing of Youth," a sermon from *The Complete Works of Matthew Henry*, 2 vols. (Edinburgh: Fullarton & Co., 1855), 2:171.

7 Van Dellen and Monsma, *The Church Order Commentary*, 78.

8 L. H. Wagenaar, *Van Strijd en Overwinning* [*Of Battle and Victory*] (Utrecht: G. J. A. Ruys, 1909), 338.

9 Elders, if they recognize the historic importance of catechism and the skill it takes to catechize, are advised to examine ministerial candidates in this area. Should deficiency be noted, elders may well urge seminaries to upgrade their training in this area.

Chapter 17: Battle Proven

1 Cited in H. Clay Trumbull, *The Sunday-School* (Philadelphia: John D. Wattles, 1893), 88.

2 John J. Murray, "Catechizing—A Forgotten Practice," *Banner of Truth* 27 (October 1962), 26.

3 Matthew Henry, "The Catechizing of Youth," a sermon from *The Complete Works of Matthew Henry*, 2 vols. (Edinburgh: Fullarton & Co., 1855), 2:163.

4 Cited in Murray, "Catechizing—A Forgotten Practice," 26.

5 Ibid.

Appendix A: Selected Confessions and Catechisms

1 John H. Leith, ed., *Creeds of the Churches* (Atlanta: John Knox Press, 1977), 127.

2 Philip Schaff, ed., *The Creeds of Christendom*, 3 vols. (reprint; Grand Rapids: Baker, 1983), 1:389–90.